KENDAL'S CANAL

HISTORY, INDUSTRY AND PEOPLE

John Satchell

Published by
**KENDAL
CIVIC
SOCIETY**

To Patricia Hovey after many years of service to Kendal as
Honorary Secretary of Kendal Civic Society
and to my wife for her constant support

Published by Kendal Civic Society

Copyright 2000 – John Satchell

First published 2000 as 'The History of the Lancaster – Kendal Canal
and its associated Industries within the Borough of Kendal'

Revised Edition 2001

Typeset in Bembo 12pt

ISBN 0 9509869 1 7

Typeset and printed by
Miller Turner Printers
The Sidings, Beezon Fields, Kendal
Tel: 01539 740937

Cover: Canal Head, late 19th century *(Margaret Duff Collection)*

CONTENTS

INTRODUCTION 5

1. HOPES AND EXPECTATIONS 9
2. THE NAVVIES 17
3. DEVELOPING THE CANAL HEAD 21

    Miller Bridge 21
    The Marble Works and Bridge Street 23
        The Marble Works 23
        The Cottages on Bridge Street 26
        The Weighing Machine 27
        The Head-Race Bridge 28
        Aynam Lodge 29
        The Builders' Yard 30
    Canal Head 31
        The Warehouses and Wharves 31
        Castle Foundry, Canal Head South 37
        Aynam Tobacco and Snuff Mills, Canal Head North 42
        Aynam Woollen Mills 46
        Canal Basin Wall 47
        Canal Head Cottage 47
        Olrig Bank 49
        Thorny Hills 49
    The Grand Opening 50

4. ACCIDENTS, LEAKAGES AND MAINTENANCE 51
5. THE PACKET BOATS AND BARGES 53
6. CASTLE MILLS TO PARR STREET 59

    The Early Mills 59
    J J & W Wilson's Mills 61
    Castle Lodge 68
    Parr Street Bridge 69

7. THE LOUND WHARVES AND THEIR
    ASSOCIATED INDUSTRIES   73
      The Gas Works   73
      The Electricity Undertaking   82
      The Three Wharves in Little Lound   83
      The Lound Foundry   85

8. CHANGE BRIDGE, IVY BANK AND
    THE CINDER FIELD   89
      Change Bridge   89
      Ivy Bank   92
      The Cinder Field   94

9. SOUTH TO THE TOWN BOUNDARY   97
      The Canal Banks   97
      The Bridges   99
      Helme Lodge   102
      Low Mills   102
      Helsington Mills   103

10. RECREATION   107

11. EFFECTS OF THE CANAL ON THE
    DEVELOPMENT OF KENDAL   113

12. THE TOWPATH WALK SOUTH –
    CANAL HEAD TO TEWITFIELD   117
      Kendal Castle   117
      The Sleddall Almshouses   118
      Parkside Road Cemetary, - a Victorian Arboretum 119
      Watercrook Roman Fort   119
      The Sedgwick Aqueduct   120
      Sedgwick House   121
      Sedgwick Gunpowder Works   121
      Hincaster Tunnel   125
      Tewitfield Locks   126
      Woods and Hedges   126

13. THE FUTURE   131

REFERENCES   133

INTRODUCTION

Kendal Civic Society originally prepared this book as a report to a South Lakeland District Council Committee (Northern Reaches Canal Management Project Team) studying proposals to bring the filled-in northern section of the Lancaster - Kendal Canal into water. The purpose of the report was to demonstrate the importance of the canal and its associated buildings as part of Kendal's industrial heritage, a purpose achieved when the Kendal Conservation Area was expanded to give the buildings the protection Conservation Area status confers.

The publicity this received resulted in a demand for the report from the general public and to meet this, the present book has been prepared in a more reader-friendly form, including a new section on features of general interest seen from the towpath as far south as the Hincaster Tunnel. From thereon various existing guides describing the Lancaster Canal take up the story.

Originally a scheme for a waterway between Kendal and the Wigan coalfield was broached as early as 1791 and the Lancashire part of the project as far south as Preston was completed by 1797. The canal did not reach Kendal however until 1819, a delay for which the inhabitants had to thank the Napoleonic war and the vast inflation it caused in construction costs(1). The general history of the canal and the detailed history of the canal basin have been well described in a number of earlier publications (see references 2, 3, 4, 5) but there is a dearth of readily available information about the industrial enterprises associated with the canal's northern reaches. There are many old industrial buildings associated with the canal, some originating before the construction of the canal in the use of the nearby River Kent for waterpower; some a direct consequence of the construction of the canal; and some from the post-canal era which found convenient sites here. It would be difficult for anyone but a few local history specialists to interpret the reasons for the layout of these surviving old buildings or to discover what their history may have been. This book aims to fill that gap and, on a wider canvas, to describe how the coming of the canal affected the development of Kendal as a manufacturing town.

Current interest in the Kendal end of the canal route centres on opening up the filled-in sections of the canal bed, bringing it into water and, via the Ribble Link, connecting it with the whole of the national canal complex south of Preston. The landscape south of Kendal is one of exceptional pastoral beauty, combining the gentle slopes and hillocks of a glaciated river valley with such dramatic limestone outcrops as Arnside and Farleton Knotts with a background to the north of the Lakeland Fells. The canal-side towpath is already providing a well-loved route out into this countryside and we hope that the insight into its industrial history and into the canal's impact on the evolution of the local landscape will enrich its enjoyment by both the boating fraternity and those using the canal for quiet waterside recreation.

Amongst the many people who have contributed information, I would like to thank Joanna Clarke (née Wilson), George Stewart, the late Angus Taylor, Geoffrey Thompson and Dr Blake Tyson, all specialists in various aspects of local history. Messrs Goodacres and United Utilities provided helpful information on their histories, Percy Duff provided many relevant photographs from the Margaret Duff Collection, Nigel Dalziel loaned photographs from the Lancaster Museums and Stephen Appleby, Trevor Hughes and British Waterways who kindly provided photographs. Jackie Fay, Kendal Library's Local History Librarian and the staff of Cumbria Record Office, Kendal, have given, as ever, their unstinting support. I thank my three Civic Society Colleagues, Michael Bottomley, John Marsh and Arthur Nicholls, who have contributed substantially from their deep knowledge of Kendal history. I also thank Anne Bonney of Helm Press whose help in assembling material, preparing the manuscript in computer format and marketing the published book is gratefully acknowledged. Finally I thank my wife who checked and polished every page of the text as it appeared and, no less important, gave sustained moral support throughout the project.

Kendal Civic Society is a registered charity (No 238470) established in 1964, with the aim of preserving the character of Kendal as a small market town "preserving the best of the old while promoting the best of the new." It has restored a number of important old buildings, promoted the construction of a new bridge across the River Kent and supported many smaller restoration schemes.

By publishing a number of guided walks leaflets and a series of local history books it seeks to raise public awareness of Kendal's heritage and so to promote its conservation. As a consequence of the publication of this canal volume the old industrial buildings associated with the canal have been brought into Kendal's Conservation Area, ensuring their better protection under planning legislation.

The author, a retired biologist turned local historian and Chairman of the Civic Society, is also author of 'Kendal on Tenterhooks' (1984), 'The Kendal Weaver' (1986) and, as co-author with Olive Wilson, 'Christopher Wilson of Kendal, an Eighteenth Century Hosier and Banker' (1988), all published by the Society. His last work, 'Family Album', Edwardian Life in the Lake Counties (1998), is an account of the photographic work of a member of a notable Kendal family of architects. The proceeds of 'Kendal's Canal, - History, Industry and People,' will go to the work of the Society.

John Satchell
Chairman
Kendal Civic Society

Aerial photograph of the Kendal end of the canal taken about 1940.

Chapter One

HOPES AND EXPECTATIONS

Before the canal was built, the Kent Valley within Kendal was already considerably industrialised with no less than five sets of mills on the river within the Borough boundaries. There existed a skilled workforce and a large reserve of labour in the surrounding countryside which the entrepreneurs of the day could expect to deploy in expanding industry around the canal.

The benefit of the canal was that it made inland transport cheaper and easier, especially for the bulk freight of industrial raw materials such as coal, metal, stone and bricks. A horse pulling a long barge could haul twenty-five tons whereas a six-ton wagon needed eight horses (6).

Road conditions around Kendal in the early 18th century were appalling. Celia Fiennes, an intrepid lady traveller, described the road south to Lancaster as *'stony and steep, far worse than the Peake in Derbyshire.'* Of the road to Bowness she wrote:

> *'Here can be noe carriages but very narrow ones like little wheelbarrows that with a horse they convey their fewell and all other things else, they also use horses on which they have a sort of pannyers ... and the reason is plaine from the narrowness of the lanes, ... Where it is hilly and stoney no other carriages can pass.'*

All this was confirmed in 1730-31 by a survey of the roads of Kendal Ward, the surveyor Benjamin Browne describing them generally as 'bad', 'narrow' or 'covered with ye hedges.'

'A View of Patterdale' John Rathbone, 1788. Goods transport before the coming of the canal

By 1800 however, all the turnpike roads out of Kendal, except the one to Levens Bridge, had been built. Reports then varied. Arthur Young in 1770 in his 'Tour of the North' wrote *'To Kendal. Turnpike. Exceeding hilly, and forme very steep, but the road itself excellent'*. The Lancaster turnpike however he found, *'Very bad, rough and cut up.'* The cumbersomeness of the vehicles as well as the poor state of the roads made travel and transport slow and hazardous compared with the smooth ride south by waterways that was to come.

Meanwhile in Lancaster and Preston canal building was the subject of hot debate. The Leeds and Liverpool Canal gained its Act of Parliament in 1770 and the following year the businessmen of Lancaster held a meeting in their Town Hall to discuss promoting a canal from Lancaster to the River Wyre. Nothing came of it and twenty years passed before a decision was finally reached in 1792 to build a canal from Kendal *via* Carnforth, Lancaster and Preston to the Wigan and Bolton coalfields, - a distance of nearly 76 miles. An enabling Act was passed by Parliament and work began the following year. By 1797 the long lock-free section from Preston to Tewitfield was opened with a great celebration and the firing of cannon in front of Lancaster Town Hall (7).

The future of the section north of Tewitfield was again debated and in 1804 the canal company confirmed its original plan to continue the canal to Kendal. Progress was slow however, the Napoleonic Wars increasing the costs of construction and reducing the supply of capital. In 1812 Thomas Cartwright, the Canal Company's engineer, estimated the cost of extending the canal to Kendal at £98,095 and in 1813 work began again with the appointment of a new Chief Engineer, Thomas Fletcher. The project was finally completed and opened in 1819, twenty-seven years after the initial decision of 1792. The cost, £600,000, was enormous in terms of the currency of the day. Kendal's White Hall, now part of the Town Hall, built around the same time in 1825, cost £6,000.

The use of the canal expected by the Lancaster Canal Committee is shown in a survey made in 1812 (Cumbria Record Office) of the goods carted the fourteen miles from Tewitfield to Kendal. It calculated the saving expected if they were to be brought by canal and the increase in demand which lower transport costs would then generate. The annual savings in transport costs of the four main categories of goods were as follows:

	£
COAL AND COAL SLACK	795
GENERAL MERCHANDISE	770
TIMBER, FREESTONE, FLAGS, BRICKS, MARBLE	500
SLATE	450
	2,515

Increase in demand, including that for goods to be forwarded beyond Kendal, was expected to yield, on average, double this sum and the demand for carriage onwards by road as far as Penrith was also expected to increase substantially. The promoters of the canal were aware that advances in 19th century agriculture, particularly in draining, would result in a steady decrease in turbary land (land from which peat or turf could be cut for fuel) and calculated that the demand for coal would therefore rise. They also expected the canal to reduce coal transport costs by three shillings a ton. Figures are not available to convert this to a proportion but in Kendal Market at that time three shillings would have bought about twelve pounds of cheese or a sack of potatoes.

The huge increase in building nationally during the Industrial Revolution produced in the late 18th century a demand for slate which was met in part by the Lakeland quarries. The Coniston quarries were at peak production in the 1790s, the slate being brought down to Greenodd for shipping. The last years of the century however saw a severe decline because of a tax levied by the Government on coastal shipping to help fund the Napoleonic War. This was equivalent to 20% of the value of Coniston and Kirkby slates and meant that the merchants could no longer compete with slates from Wales (8).

The canal operating from Kendal was expected to reduce the cost of slate and increase demand and this proved justified. In 1819 Coniston's slate industry improved when the new waterway linked Kendal with Lancashire and allowed considerable transport economies when compared with coastal shipping. There was little difference in the cost of carting from Coniston to Kendal and carting and boating from Coniston to Greenodd. On the other hand, savings made by avoiding the coastal shipping tax were significant. Soon carts loaded with slate were leaving Coniston, trundling over the fells to Kendal and the canal terminus.

When the Preston to Tewitfield section of the Lancaster Canal was opened in 1797 a boat loaded with limestone was towed from Tewitfield to Galgate and ceremonially exchanged for a boat-load of coal, this section of the waterway subsequently becoming known as 'the Black and White Canal'. At a later date a tramline was built from the limestone quarries on Farleton Knott to the canal at Crooklands but there seems little evidence of export of limestone via the canal from Kendal. The Kendal trade directory for 1829 lists the 'Lime Masters' who supplied lime and suppliers of slate, flagstones and 'marble' but makes no mention of a trade in limestone for building purposes.

Cheap coal also facilitated the production of burned limestone for making mortar, increasingly in demand as the building boom accelerated. Extensive lime burning took place on Kendal Fell after 1820, a fine kiln surviving today on the edge of the former quarry.

Records of lime burning on Kendal Fell begin with the Kendal Fell Trust's Act of 1767 which gave property owners in Kendal "*the Right and Liberty of ... getting Limestone and burning the same into lime.*" As the Trust's minute books contain no further reference to it before 1823 lime burning must have been on a small scale, almost certainly using wood as fuel. After the arrival of the canal however there are numerous references to it in the minutes. They include the rents of the kilns and their tenants; charges levied on the amount of lime sold; the failure of the lime burners to keep proper accounts and pay their rents on time; obstruction of Beast Banks by '*choking the Green with (their) horses and carts*'; and the lime burners burning the fences as fuel. The chaotic manner in which the quarrymen extracted the limestone and disposed of the spoil produced further problems (40). The trade directory for 1829 (9) records six 'Lime Masters', all operating on Kendal Fell.

Besides these minute book entries there are records in the local newspapers of deaths by sulphur gas poisoning in 1833 and 1834. One of the victims found dead in a kiln had been a former employee; the other was a tramp who had gone to the edge of a kiln for warmth to sleep and was overcome by the sulphur before catching fire.

Steel lime burner, Pennington's quarry.   *Margaret Duff Collection*

Lime kiln, Greenside, Kendal. *G. V. Berry*

In 1863 the Kendal Fell Trustees were discussing building and operating a new limekiln. A cost analysis prepared for the Trustees shows that coke, not coal, was the preferred fuel, a product not only of the gas works but also of the coke ovens on Cinder Field, adjacent to Change Bridge. All of these records point to a rapid and sustained growth in the production of lime for mortar used in the building boom which followed the opening of the canal.

Lime for agricultural use was usually burned in small kilns on large farm estates, particularly for sweetening newly enclosed land. Wood was often used for fuel where it was freely available and many kilns were built along the Westmorland Limestone belt from Underbarrow to Kirkby Lonsdale after the arrival of the canal in Kendal (1).

The expectations of the Canal Committee concerning goods to be forwarded by road were confirmed after the warehouses were built in that their first lease, in 1827, was to James Machell, a common carrier. The 1829 trade directory (9) confirmed the importance of the canal in bringing coal to Kendal, the occupants of the Canal Basin then being seven coal merchants and three slate merchants. In 1840, 193,000 tons of coal were carried to Canal Head. The 1849 trade directory (10) shows seven out of nine coal merchants and one slate yard still operating from the canal.

The take-over of the canal trade by the railways became a serious prospect in 1831 when an Act of Parliament was passed to allow the building of the Wigan to Preston Railway which opened as the North Union Railway in 1834. The Lancaster and Preston Junction Railway opened in 1840 and by 1846 the Lancaster and Carlisle Railway was running trains between Carlisle and Preston. By 1850 the canal was carrying only heavy goods and coal while the railway carried passengers and light merchandise.

In 1857 the Lancaster and Carlisle Railway was taken over by the London and North Western Railway which in 1864 also took a lease of the canal from Preston to Kendal in perpetuity for £12,600 a year. In 1885 the LNWR bought the canal company outright and the trade

Filling in the canal near the Borough boundry, 1962. *Margaret Duff Collection.*

directory of that year (11) shows five out of sixteen coal merchants still operating from the canal, eight of the others having yards at the railway station. By then there were no slate yards still operating from the canal.

In 1923 the London Midland and Scottish Railway bought out the LNWR, including the Lancaster Canal, which in 1944, it sought to close. By this date the canal was used only by boats delivering coal to the gasworks and even this ended in the autumn of 1944 when coal delivery was taken over by road transport. In 1948 the canal was nationalised and in 1955 was classified as 'having insufficient commercial prospects to justify its retention'. The section from Stainton into Kendal was closed down and the top two miles were filled-in.

View of Kendal about 1820. Engraving by Allom & Rose

Chapter Two

THE NAVVIES

When the canal had reached Hincaster but work towards Kendal had yet to begin, the town was already feeling the impact of the navvies. On 5th July 1817, the Westmorland Advertiser reported that a number of the labourers;

> *'amongst whom were several disorderly Irishmen, had remained in town all night and had committed several outrages the next day ... such as calling for drink and taking fruit from the stalls in the street and then refusing to pay. Their conduct at the Wheatsheaf in Kirkland was outrageous in the extreme for, besides injuring the doors and windows, they forced the landlord (who was sick) from his bed and dragged him about the floor by his heels, besides maltreating his wife in a most inhuman manner. Two of these lawless ruffians were taken into custody, after a stout resistance, during which a Constable received a violent contusion.'*

The Advertiser thought '*They should be held up as an example to the unruly multitude which the cutting of the canal will shortly bring into this populous neighbourhood.*' They got six months.

Three months later the Advertiser (25th October 1817) reported another outrage. Richard Payne, a dyer, was attacked on the road by a navvie '*who with a short shillaly knocked him down and demanded his money. Finding he had none he kicked and beat him and grasping his heels over his shoulders dragged him thirty or forty yards along the road.*'

Alarming though these incidents were they were on a small scale compared with the electioneering violence of February 1818 when Lord and Colonel Lowther visited Kendal to canvass support for the Tories. Rashly, free ale was distributed in the town centre the night before, the drinking continuing till midnight. Next morning the navvies got a barrel to themselves and when the local Tory supporters assembled to welcome the Lowther Party, pelted them with mud and stones through the town and out along the Milnthorpe Road. A mob about five hundred strong set up barricades at Nether Bridge in the path of the Lowther party which comprised one hundred and thirty-one horsemen, eleven carriages and the yeomanry.

After repeated assaults the horsemen broke through and Lord Lowther in his battered carriage was allowed to reach the town centre where he escaped into the King's Arms. The navvies threatened to pull the building down but were persuaded with bribes of more beer to move to the Commercial Inn and then to the White Hart. In a drunken riot they climbed in and out of the windows, ate two Cheshire cheeses, pulled the furniture to pieces and left the ground floor virtually gutted (12). It must have been a relief to the magistrates, if not to Kendal in general, when the canal was completed.

In recalling these events allowance should be made for the conditions under which the men worked and lived. Farm outbuildings were often used as lodgings or, where many men were concentrated as at the Lune Aqueduct, camps of primitive lodgings were built.

The cutting of a canal started with making a trench about twenty feet wide and seven feet deep, the men alternating the jobs of picking, shovelling and wheeling the laden barrows up wooden planks to the surface. The bottom and sides of the trench were then waterproofed with a lining of a special hydraulic clay made from volcanic ash imported from the neighbourhood of Pozzuoli in Italy which developed cement-like properties when wetted. The men had to stamp this down to drive out trapped pockets of air. Sometimes cattle were driven in and chased up and down to do this job (13). The men worked a ten hour day, often more, six days a week and could expect to earn two shillings and two pence per day, more than double the rate for agricultural labourers at the time, if, that is, they had the stamina to do the work on a diet of mainly bread, cheese and beer. Tough though it was, it was preferable to the drudgery of the cotton mills where small children were still working a sixteen hour day.

Navvies, originally the 'navigators' who built the canals, worked in gangs which moved on from one job to another. Peter Lecount, a railway builder described them in 1835 as:

> *'the terror of the surrounding country; they are as completely a class by themselves as the gypsies. Possessed of all the daring recklessness of the smuggler, without any of his redeeming qualities, their ferocious behaviour can only be equalled by the brutality of their language.'*

The riotous brawls associated with the navvies in Kendal have to be viewed in the wider context of the rising militancy of the reform movement in the north generally in the early 19th century. With its dependence on waterpower and the obsolete technology of its textile industry; the poverty of its handloom weavers, and its variety of anti-establishment religious beliefs, protest and riot were nothing new to Kendal. The opening of the Kendal canal preceded by a mere two months the Peterloo Massacre in Manchester when the Hussars armed with sabres were let loose by the magistrates on a huge open-air reform meeting, leaving eleven dead and about four hundred wounded.

MAP OF THE HISTORIC BUILDINGS
AROUND THE CANAL HEAD

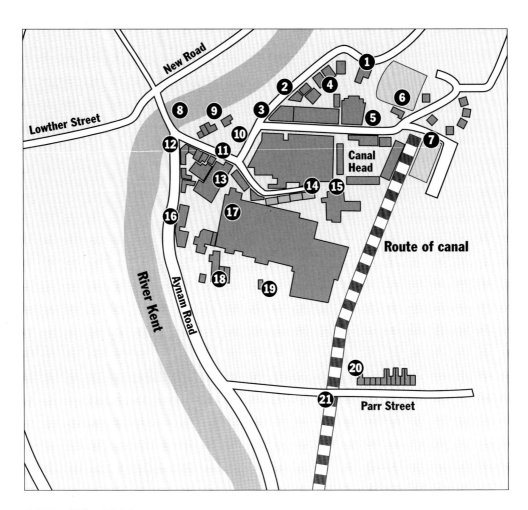

KEY TO MAP

1. Olrig Bank
2. Aynam Woollen Mill Gatehouse
3. Aynam Mills
4. Engine House and Chimney
5. Kendal Brown House
6. Canal Head Manager's Cottage
7. Canal Wall
8. Miller Bridge
9. Aynam Lodge
10. Gilbert Gilkes and Gordon's Premises
11. Head-Race Parapet
12. Bridge House and 3-7 Bridge Street
13. Castle Mills Dye House
14. Converted Industrial Buildings
15. Castle Foundry
16. Goodacres' Premises
17. Castle Mills and Engine Shed
18. Castle Lodge and Cottages
19. Gardener's Cottage
20. Sunnyside House with Datestone
21. Parr Street Bridge and Steps

Chapter Three

DEVELOPING THE CANAL HEAD

MILLER BRIDGE

The first step in building the canal terminus was to replace the narrow bridge to Castle Mills, built in 1743, with a new wider bridge which would in the short term carry the construction traffic and later serve the Canal Head and Castle Mills traffic. On 13th April 1818 the Canal Committee instructed the Kendal architect, Alderman Francis Webster, to prepare plans. By the 20th May 1818 the specifications had been completed, tenders submitted, contracts let and the foundation stone laid. By November the work was complete and the bridge, spanning one

Alderman Francis Webster, Architect. Designer of Miller Bridge and the Canal Head complex.
Kendal Town Hall Collection

Alderman Thomas Harrison, Surgeon. Mayor of Kendal 1805-6, 1815-6, 1828-9 and Secretary to the Kendal Canal Committee.
Kendal Town Hall Collection

Miller Bridge.

Miller Bridge datestone.

hundred and fifty feet in three arches, and including an approach from Lowther Street of dressed stone pillars and iron railings, was opened to traffic.

On 1st April 1820, the Westmorland Advertiser carried a report of the presentation of a silver gilt cup to the secretary of the Kendal Canal Committee, Alderman Thomas Harrison, '*As a compliment for valuable and unremitting services in promoting the interest of the town in the construction of the new bridge over the River Kent and the warehouses of the canal basin.*' The bridge survives in its original form together with Webster's approach railings and pillars.

Miller Bridge south western approach railings.

THE MARBLE WORKS AND BRIDGE STREET

The Marble Works
Bridge Street was developed next with the Websters' marble works on
the corner between Bridge Street and the road to Castle Mills. Aynam
Road was not built until 1877. The marble works housed the
showrooms, the town office and some of the equipment and stores of
their factory down-river at Low Mills. The 1829 directory (9) states:

> *'The Marble Works in the town (Kendal) and neighbourhood belonging
> to George and Francis Webster, are very extensive and were first brought
> into repute by the late Mr (Francis) Webster, architect who, about thirty
> years ago, constructed machinery on the River Kent for sawing and
> polishing marble ….In the town Messrs Webster have their splendid
> showrooms for manufactured chimney pieces, etc. The surrounding district
> supplies the finest black and other marbles and the advantage possessed
> by Kendal of sea and inland navigation facilities facilitate the*

Bridge House

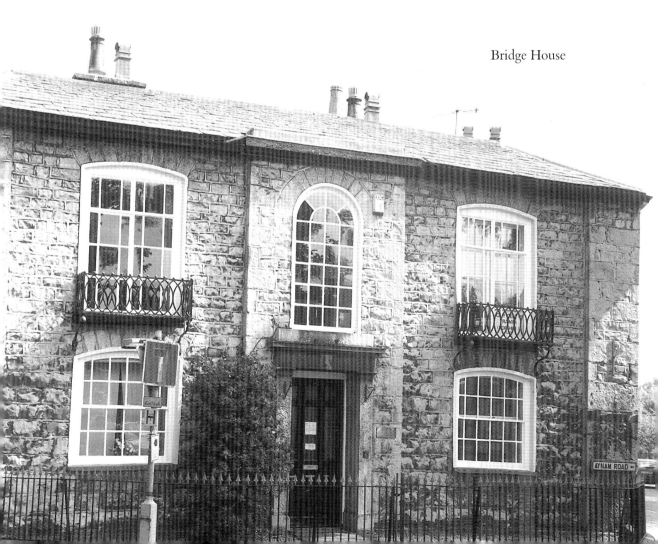

importation of Italian marble to be manufactured and re-shipped to most of the principal towns in the Kingdom.'

The phrase 'inland navigation facilities' clearly indicates the use of the canal for this trade. Sea navigation is again referred to in the 1829 directory which notes that 'Carriers by Water' from the Canal Head warehouse included *'James Widner's vessels, the Thomas, William and Dee which convey goods from Hest Bank to Liverpool.'* Prior to the building of the Glasson branch, Hest Bank was a busy transhipment point for goods between the canal and the sea.

The location of the marble works on the River Kent is confirmed by Cornelius Nicholson in his 'Annals of Kendal' (14):

'About the year 1800… Mr Webster erected machinery at Low Mills, on the River Kent, for sawing and polishing marble.'

Francis Webster's earliest known work in Kendal is the obelisk dated 1788 on Castle Howe, built in partnership with a mason, William Holme, from premises at the west end of New Inn Yard. Almost thirty

years later when Francis was an Alderman and architect to the Canal Committee, he was in an advantageous position to take a lease on part of Miller's Close, a prime development site between the east end of Miller Bridge and the developing canal head. Here, with access to the canal for shipping in foreign marble and shipping out heavy manufactured goods, Francis and his two sons George and Francis developed their business.

A Webster 'chimney piece' from Thorny Hills, Kendal. *Angus Taylor*

The Canal Committee's minute book records the lease in October 1818 and the completion of Miller's Close marble works by 1819. By 1828 the business was described in Pigott's trade directory as *'Francis Webster and Sons. Architects, Sculptors and manufacturers of Italian and British chimney pieces by machinery'*.

Local patrons were able to visit the Miller's Close showroom to see the choice of material and designs available. The diary of the second Earl of Burlington for whom Webster was enlarging Holker Hall records a drive over to Kendal to select chimney pieces from the showroom. W. D. Crewdson bought two for Helme Lodge. A *'dining room chimney piece of black marble with full fluted Ionic Columns'* cost twenty five shillings in 1827 and another in *'Beetham Marble'* cost thirty five shillings (30). Aynam Lodge, another Webster house, had one, *'with Doric columns in black and coloured marbles'*.

After Francis's death, his sons opened showrooms in Liverpool, Preston and probably Manchester, the Kendal historian Cornelius Nicholson commenting in 1861:

> *'the works of art, scattered throughout the Kingdom, with numerous sepulchral monuments and specimens of architectural skill, which adorn this town and neighbourhood in particular will long bear honourable testimony to his (Francis's) merit'.*

The Websters' business interests were not however confined to architecture, monuments and chimney pieces but extended to quarrying roofing slate. Slate was quarried for landowners and to cover the buildings designed in the firm's architectural department. Indeed, in his definitive work on the Websters, Taylor quotes a letter from George Webster to the Earl of Burlington stating that he would have given up architecture were it not for the fact that it sold slate. The 1829 trade directory lists as slate merchants George and Francis Webster of Kent Side, Bridge Street, presumably the Marble Works.

From 1814 until about this date Francis Webster rented Wrangle Gill quarries at the head of Long Sleddale from the Howards of Levens Hall but, following disputes over the management of the quarry, the Websters moved to the largest of three quarries at Kirkby Ireleth, north west of Ulverston and owned by the Cavendishes of Holker. In 1750 Bishop Pocock noted in a diary of his travels that at Kirkby *'they have a light slate which is esteemed the best in England'*. The slate was displayed at the Kendal Marble Works, a Webster advertisement of 1842 *'begging to inform their friends and the public of a regular assortment of dark blue Lancashire slates in the Marble Yard at Kendal... ...also at Canal Head, Ulverston and at the quarries at Kirkby Ireleth'.*

The Websters employed Thomas Duckett to manage their sculpture depatment, his best known works in Kendal being the figure of St. George on the east front of the church of Holy Trinity, St. George and the bust of Vitellio in Abbot Hall Art Gallery and, in Preston, the statue of Sir Robert Peel in Winkley Square, carved from Kendal Fell limestone.

The main front of the original showroom has survived almost intact although an iron balcony on the Aynam Road side has been lost.

The Cottages on Bridge Street

A further minute, for 18th November 1830, records the conversion of part of the Marble Works to a dwelling. The population census of 1841 shows this dwelling as occupied by Mr Francis Webster, aged 35... i.e. Francis Webster junior. Now No 3 Bridge Street, its stylish doorway shows classical details much in vogue with the Websters in the 1830s and the highly decorative doorway and reduced window squeezed into the otherwise symmetrical northern elevation suggest that No 3 is that conversion.

No. 3 Bridge Street.

The minutes also record proposals to build cottages on Bridge Street designed by Frances Webster and their completion in 1822. Nos 4, 4a and 5 Bridge Street appear to be of that date. They have modern doors and windows, having been renovated recently. No 7, of later 19th century date, is a private dwelling, the property of Messrs Goodacre. It retains its original front elevation. A fire station was built on part of the Marble Works site on Aynam Road at around the turn of the century.

No's 3-5 Bridge Street.

The Weighing Machine

Between No 5 and No 7 Bridge Street, where a garage now stands, was the site of the Canal Head weighing machine.

Two months after the canal opened the Committee prepared a set of charges for its use, listing the goods expected to be handled as follows:

HAY	4d	PER CART
MERCHANT COALS	2d	" "
COALS	1d	" "
STRAW	2d	" "
MANURE	2d	" "
WOOD	2d	" "
SLATE	1d	" "

Two-horse carts were charged double

The 1841 population census returns show a sixty-year old 'weigher', Robert Shaw, and his wife giving 'Weighing Machine' as their address, presumably living on the premises.

The Head-Race Bridge

As part of the 1818 plans, Francis Webster prepared a design for a three-arched bridge on Bridge Street to allow water to pass to the Castle Mills water wheels. On representations from Castle Mills, a fourth arch was added. The head-race having been filled in, only the parapet walls can now be seen. The bridge originally had a flared approach at both ends of the parapets, the coping stones terminating with special capstones. The north parapet retains this original form at its east end. The west end has been altered but retains its capstone. The south parapet has been altered at both ends.

The bridge over the head-race, about 1900. *Margaret Duff Collection*

The north parapet of the head-race bridge

Aynam Lodge

This substantial house, designed by Webster, was built in 1823 for
Thomas Harrison, a surgeon, whose name is shown on the property on
Wood's map of 1833. The single-storey wing on the south, now called
Aynam Cote, was his surgery which he could reach from his front door

under the cover of
a veranda, now
removed, which
faced what is now
Gilkes' car park.
The coach house
and stables at the
north end of the
garden are now
occupied as
offices. The house
was subsequently
the home of Titus
Wilson, printer,
bookbinder, and
bookseller.

Aynam Lodge. West elevation

The Builders' Yard

In the late 19th and early 20th centuries, what is now Gilkes' car park was occupied as a builders' yard, initially by James Howie, mason and builder.

Howie's Yard.   *Margaret Duff Collection*

CANAL HEAD

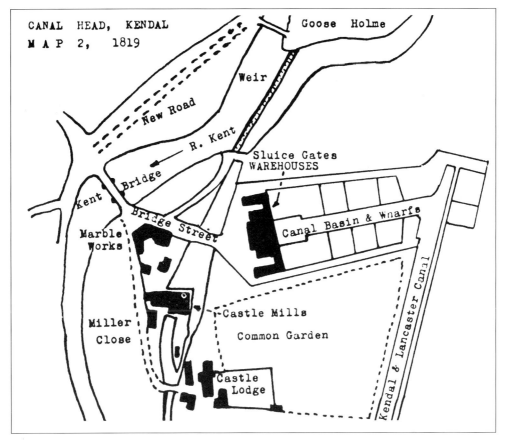

Plan of Canal Head, 1819.   *P N Wilson 1968*

The Warehouses and Wharves

The history of Canal Head has already been well described (4,5). To summarize, on the west side of the canal terminus, the Corporation built a canal basin with four wharves each on its north and south sides, two wharves at its east end, and a pair of covered warehouses along its west end. Each warehouse was fifty-five feet by sixty feet with an arch in the eastern wall through which the barges floated to the covered wharves. In the western wall were large doorways opening onto loading bays facing Bridge Street. Flanking these bays were a stable block on the north side and some cottages on the south side, completed in 1819.

The railway came to Kendal in 1846 and the canal rapidly became uneconomic. The Corporation responded by closing off the end of the canal basin with a wall backed with puddled clay, leaving the warehouses dry and available for new uses. The first new tenant, in 1854, was a local timber merchant who converted his part of the premises into a sawmill, powered by steam.

Gilbert Gilkes, Turbine Manufacturer.
Mayor of Kendal 1898-1901
Kendal Town Hall Collection

A new lease was drawn in 1856 between the Corporation and William and Henry Williamson of Stainton, general engineers, who converted the southern warehouse into an iron foundry, 'The Canal Iron Works'. The northern section became a machine and fitting shop. They made all sorts of machines for the local bobbin mills and sawmills, threshing and other agricultural machines and steam engines but soon became known for their 'Vortex'

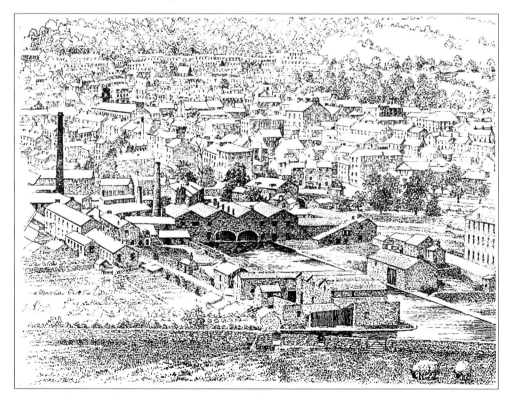

The Canal Basin, drawn by A. Wainwright from a photograph taken about 1881

water-turbines, built to the design of Professor James Thompson of Queen's College, Belfast. In 1881, the firm was bought by Gilbert Gilkes. The surviving stone chimney is believed to have been built by the Williamsons in or shortly after 1856. A history of Gilbert Gilkes and Gordon has been written by P N Wilson (5).

The District Valuer's 1912 maps and 1910 ledgers throw some light on the use to which the wharves and buildings were put at that later date. The whole of the warehouse block facing Bridge Street is recorded as owned by Gilbert Gilkes and Company, and shown on the map as Canal Iron Works. Three of the four wharves on Canal Head North were still occupied by coal merchants – the Wigan Coal and Iron Company, Samuel Thompson and Company, who also operated from

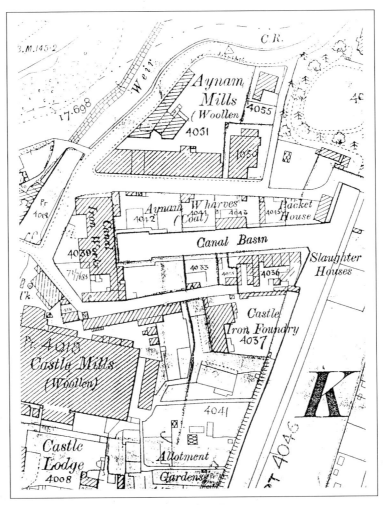

Canal Head. Detail from District Valuer's map, 1912

the railway station, and Anthony Thompson, both with stables there. John Hine, a stonemason, occupied the most easterly wharf, shown on the map as adjacent to the Packet House. The Wigan Coal and Iron Company had a stable and a stone yard on Canal Head South. At the east end of Canal Head South, on the north side, were the Corporation's slaughter houses and a workshop and yard occupied by a butcher. When a new Corporation abattoir in Sandylands was completed in 1932, the Mayor opened the proceedings by personally slaughtering a pig (3).

The west elevation of the warehouses has been greatly altered with successive extensions of the buildings westwards concealing the original 1819 front. The wing projecting north onto Canal Head North, believed to have been the original office, has a Venetian window on the upper floor.

The building curving around the northwest corner of Canal-Head South is today exactly as shown on the Ordnance Survey map of 1858, some small modern blocks excluded. The engine house and chimney are also shown on the 1858 Ordnance Survey map. From Canal Head South the arch of the filled-in opening between the Canal Head Foundry and its yard can be seen.

Canal Head Foundry chimney and archway of goods exit from the original south warehouse.   *Stephen Appleby*

Wing on Canal Head North
believed to have been the
original packet boat office

Castle Foundry

Castle Foundry, Canal Head South

The history of this iron foundry is summarised on the letterhead of Day's Iron Foundry when it was established in Kendal as the Castle Foundry. 'Established as Winder & Heaton at Lancaster in 1703. Removed to Crooklands near Kendal 1750; Gatebeck near Kendal 1818; Low Mills, Kendal 1826; Lound Foundry, Kendal 1850; Castle Foundry, Kendal 1893.'

A news item of 24th December 1892, reported:

> *New Foundry in Kendal. The piece of land situated between Castle Mills and the Lancaster Canal has been purchased by Mr Day of the Lound Foundry and plans for a new building are in the hands of Mr Stephen Shaw. Mr Day will remove his plant and patterns to the new premises as soon as they are ready and as the position is so central and convenient, no doubt a much larger trade will result.*

H H Day moved to the Castle Foundry in 1893. It was built for him by George Martindale, a Kendal builder who also constructed for him a five ton jib crane, using Day's own castings. The foundry had two cupolas, a core-drying oven with a sliding steel door, and an upper floor of cast iron plates carried in T-girders with horse manure as insulation. The cupolas or furnaces were used to melt scrap iron or pig iron, limestone and coke being added by the furnace man until the iron began to run (15).

Castle Foundry datestone

The two cupolas at Day's Foundry.   *Margaret Duff Collection*

The foundry produced grates, L-shaped boilers, gully grates, stop taps and covers, toffee boilers, cast-iron milestones, stanchions, and other small items. A grating giving access to a drain with H. H. DAY CASTLE FOUNDRY KENDAL in relief has survived west of the foundry in the adjacent entrance to Gilkes on the south side of Canal Head South. The foundry also cast gunmetal. It closed in 1938 and Gilkes purchased the site. Although the foundry no doubt used the canal for despatching goods and importing iron and coke, in the 20th century it also sent goods to the railway station by horse and cart (16).

Grating cast at Day's Foundry
Anne Bonney

There are two former Castle Mills warehouses on Canal Head South, now converted to dwellings. East of these is the shell of Day's Foundry with, on its north wall, 'Castle Foundry, 1893' in deep relief. There are no original internal structures surviving but the building is still in industrial use.

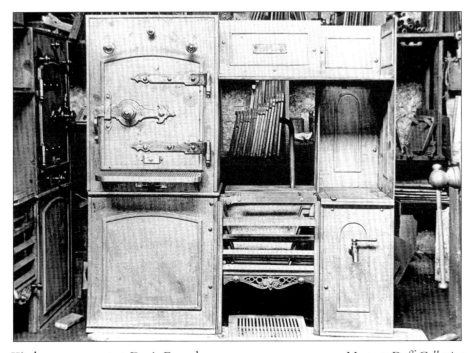

Kitchen range cast at Day's Foundry.   *Margaret Duff Collection*

Casting at Day's Foundry
John Marsh Collection

The later expansion of the industrial buildings at Canal Head and Castle Mills is illustrated on the 1938 and 1994 maps below which are based on Ordnance Survey data.

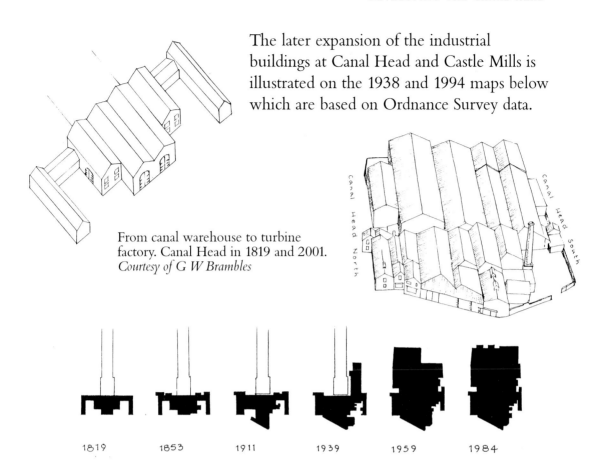

From canal warehouse to turbine factory. Canal Head in 1819 and 2001.
Courtesy of G W Brambles

1819   1853   1911   1939   1959   1984

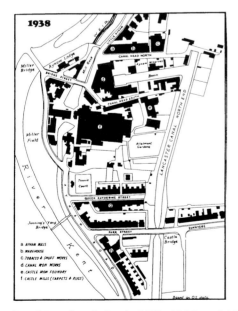
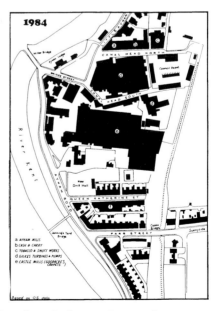

Canal Head and Castle Mills 1938 and 1984. Based on Ordnance Survey data.
Courtesy of G W Brambles

Aynam Tobacco and Snuff Mills, Canal Head North
Snuff manufacture began in Kendal in 1792 when Thomas Harrison brought tobacco equipment to Mealbank. His daughter married Samuel Gawith who continued the business, the couple living at 29 Lowther Street until Samuel's death in 1865. Two of their sons John and Samuel II, then ran the business until 1878 when they dissolved the partnership. Samuel II then formed a new company, Samuel Gawith and Company, and built a new tobacco factory at Canal Head. This was expanded in 1936 and snuff-grinding machinery was transferred to the new premises, their business continuing today in 'Kendal Brown House'.

Samuel Gawith the First, Snuff Manufacturer. Mayor of Kendal 1864-5. *Kendal Town Hall Collection*

John Thomas Illingworth, an employee of Samuel Gawith 1st, set up a small tobacco business off Highgate in 1867, later moving to part of Samuel Gawith 2nd's premises on Canal Head North (17). Illingworth's produced only snuff after 1931, becoming the country's largest manufacturer and exporter.

The business closed in 1983 when fire destroyed the machinery and gutted the building.

Notwithstanding the extensive fire damage to the building on the corner of Canal Head North and Little Aynam it has been rebuilt to a high standard and forms an important element in the street scene. The adjacent warehouse on its east side, formerly occupied by John W Carlisle, is externally very much in its original condition with three stories with six windows in each. At the rear, facing the mill yard, are the warehouse doors on each floor and at the east end a wing projecting north with a gantry hoist in the gable and a factory clock. The whole is limestone built with dressed quoins.

Northeast on Canal Head North are two more warehouses built with a

Samuel Gawith the Second. Founder of the Canal Head tobacco firm, Samuel Gawith and Company

Making twist, Illingworth's about 1920.   *Margaret Duff Collection*

continuous frontage. The first also has three floors and six windows per floor, and the second has a semicircular-headed doorway and nine windows.

The burnt out mill 1983(3)

Aynam Mills, west elevation

Kendal Brown
House

Kendal Brown House, east of the warehouses, also appears much as originally built with a semicircular door, with an inscribed keystone. It has a particularly good panelled front door. At the rear of Kendal Brown House is an engine house and a well maintained octagonal factory chimney built in dressed limestone.

Chimney at rear of
Kendal Brown House

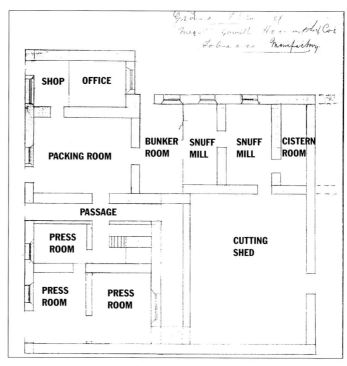

Ground plan of Kendal Brown House
(*Cumbria Record Office/WDB35/Plan 404*)

Aynam Woollen Mills
North of Aynam Snuff Mills on Little Aynam, the 1897 Ordnance Survey map shows Aynam Woollen Mills, founded by George J McKay, described in Kelly's Directory of 1873 as a woollen merchant and horse-clothing manufacturer of Kent Street. In the 1855 Directory he is described as "woollen horse rug, brace and belt manufacturer." His house, Olrig Bank, a few yards along Little Aynam, has a spouthead dated 1879 and this is probably close to the date of the factory. George McKay's son, George Mills McKay, was educated at Heversham, became Sheriff of London in 1921-22, a founder of the English Speaking Union and received a knighthood (18).

In 1910 the factory premises were divided between the mill, occupied by McKay & Company and the warehouse portion, occupied by J D Ramsay &

Aynam Woollen Mills

George McKay, Woollen Manufacturer. Mayor of Kendal 1890-1. *Kendal Town Hall Collection*

Company, a firm of baby linen manufacturers. The former single-storey gatehouse is in considerable disrepair but retains something of its original charm. At eaves level it has a row of corbels on both sides, carved in gritstone in a fluted scroll design, now mostly weathered beyond recognition. The premises are now converted to a garage.

Canal Basin Wall, Canal Head North
The northern edge of the Canal Basin is visible to a depth of about two feet just inside the perimeter fence of the South Lakeland District Council Storage Depot. The coping stones are joined with iron ties.

Canal Basin retaining wall

Canal Head Cottage
John Wood's map of 1833 shows a rectangular building on the north side of Canal Head North, a short distance northwest of the head of the canal. This building still exists, albeit with modern extensions. Formerly known as 'The Agent's House', it is believed to have been occupied by the Agent of the Canal Company. It served in more recent times as the Kendal Girls' High School caretaker's house. The house has been extended on its east side but otherwise preserves its original appearance largely unchanged.

Canal Head Cottage, about 1900.   *John Marsh Collection*

Another building which stood at the end of Canal Head North on the east side of the beginning of the towpath was demolished within living memory. The photograph shows a sign which reads 'W. Vickers' Brick and Coal Yard. Dealer in Hay and Straw.' William Vickers of Canal Head has an entry with much the same wording in Bulmer's trade directory of 1885. It illustrates the continued use of the canal for bulk freight haulage long after the date when the canal had been bought out by the railway.

Vickers' coal office. The costume of the man wearing a straw hat suggests a date of about 1900   *Trevor Hughes Collection*

Olrig Bank, Little Aynam

Built for the original owner of the woollen mill this house is little altered from its original appearance. It has a cast iron spout head with the date 1879 and is one of the few Victorian houses in Kendal with its cast iron roof ridge decoration surviving.

Thorny Hills

Having completed the construction of Canal Head, Francis Webster had the foresight to see that the rough hilly ground overlooking the River Kent from the east had potential as a superior housing site. At a meeting of the local Canal Committee in 1821 he proposed building a 'Range of Houses' there and was asked the following year to mark out the ground. Plots were sold by the Corporation at two shillings a square yard, each potential purchaser being required to submit his own plan. The 'Local Chronology' reported that *'When finished the Thorny Hills will be the most elegant promenade in the neighbourhood'*. George Webster built a grand house there, No 4 for his own occupation and his brother Francis bought No 6 in 1852 (41).

Olrig Bank
Stephen Appleby

THE GRAND OPENING

The first boat reached the Canal Head basin on the 4th April, 1819. A few days later the embankment burst some seven miles south of Kendal and the opening planned for the 1st May had to be postponed. By the 18th June however the burst had been repaired and the canal and its associated works were ready for a grand ceremonial opening. Killington Reservoir had been constructed to feed the canal down Crooklands Beck, a leak in the dam had been repaired and stray horses and cows had been rounded up off the towpath. Flags were hoisted on the principal buildings, cannons were procured to fire at intervals through the morning and lookouts were posted at the bridges. Kendal Corporation and their ladies embarked on the Corporation barge, followed by another barge filled with gaily attired occupants, the bells rang and a start was made towards Lancaster to meet the contingent expected from the Lancaster Committee. The bands played, the cannon fired and the procession of five barges and three packet boats set off at about ten o'clock reaching Hincaster tunnel at twelve and Crooklands at one o'clock. Joining up with the party from Lancaster, the full procession of sixteen boats arrived back at Kendal at about five o'clock to the cheers of some ten thousand people packed onto Castle Hill. After an evening of dining and speeches the festivities concluded with a ball attended by about a hundred people (12).

Kendal Basin in 1897   *Courtesy of Mairi Miller*

Chapter Four

ACCIDENTS, LEAKAGES AND MAINTENANCE

There were occasional drownings in the canal. A new-born infant was found in the water in 1820; a John Strickland was drowned in 1821; a bargee's child sailing with a load of limestone from Kendal fell overboard and drowned in the locks at Tewitfield in 1823; and in the same year a Kendal resident, intending to meet the packet boat, fell into the water at Canal Head on a dark night and narrowly escaped drowning. The Westmorland Advertiser responded with a call for the canal basin to be railed and for better lighting on the approach to it.

In March 1885 a young man was drowned in the canal near the gasworks. The Westmorland Gazette commented:

> *'The dragnet near the spot should be speedily replaced. It is too heavy to be of use to a drowning man. It is fit to hold a bull and if it struck a person in the water it would kill rather than save – it is described as life saving apparatus.'*

Lifebelts were placed at Canal Head and the gasworks a few months later.

Several of the drownings were ascribed in the Coroner's reports (Public Record Office) to various degrees of drunkenness. A platelayer found dead in the canal in 1890 was described as having been seen '*not quite sober*'; the young man drowned in 1885 was said to have been seen coming out of a public house '*not sober*' and a man found drowned under Highgate Settlings Bridge (Burton Road) in 1883 was last seen '*very drunk*'.

A rescue was reported in the Westmorland Gazette of 1887 as follows:

> 'There was a fortunate rescue from drowning in the canal last Saturday night. Three proficient swimmers who had swum the long bridge length near Helme Lodge were measuring the distance on the banks. A gurgling noise was heard in the canal and, on looking about, they saw a pitiable object all but drowned in the water. After some trouble a farmer from New Hutton was hauled out in a very exhausted state. When he had come round and was able to speak, he told his rescuers that he had fallen asleep on the bank, and that rolling into the water had "wakkened him up!" He was struggling in the deep water when his rescuers heard him.'

Suicide drownings were recorded as 'suicide during temporary insanity' or some similar wording. Various accidents, - children falling through the ice, falling overboard or drowned while bathing – contributed to the canal's death toll.

The canal was closed and emptied from time to time at various points to repair leakages, clear out rubbish and construct new structures. A strong leakage at Watercrook was repaired in May 1879 and a pipe was laid under the canal to accommodate an undercurrent. In 1884 gales washed out puddled clay and caused leakages and in 1890 a leakage was reported as being dangerous to workers in the Canal Iron Works at Canal Head.

In 1882 the growth of waterweed in the canal was heavier than for several years and over a distance of sixty miles, thirty men were occupied in clearing it for four weeks. In that year the canal was closed while a wall against the water at Lound Wharf, was rebuilt by the Corporation. The Company put in a new wharf wall against the water north of Parr Street Bridge and cleared out all the weed and rubbish from the length towards Canal Head. While the water was being drained off the previous night, a man stepped into the water with a bag and pole to catch fish at the trunk valve. The strong current drew him into the eighteen inch diameter pipe down which he was carried about forty yards and drowned (Public Record Office).

> 'I must get out of these wet clothes and into a dry martini.'
> Alexander Woolcott

Chapter Five

THE PACKET BOATS
AND BARGES

The packet boat service opened for business in June 1819, carrying passengers and parcels between Kendal and Lancaster every weekday. A decade later, the 1829 directory states that:

> 'The Kent and Lune Packet Boats sail from the canal alternately every day except Sundays for Lancaster and Preston, etc. to convey passengers and parcels and arrives at Kendal at 9 evg'.

Initially the office for the packet services is believed to have been in the wing of the Canal Head building with a Venetian window on the upper floor which projects into Canal Head North (see page 36). A late 19th century photograph in the Margaret Duff Collection which is too dark to reproduce shows it signed as the office of the Wigan Coal and Iron Company however. A gable at the rear of this wing bears the date 1891. On Hoggarth's map of 1853 a new building is shown on the west bank of the Canal Head which is absent from the 1819 and 1833 maps and on the District Valuer's map of 1912 this is shown as the 'Packet House'. It was probably built in 1833 when a new service was begun but John Wood's map had already been drawn.

The boats were seventy feet long and six feet wide, with a thin iron hull that weighed less than 1.75 tons and a loaded draught of 16.75 inches. To save weight, covered cabin and steerage accommodation was provided by stretching oiled cloth over curved ribs, with spaces left for windows. In cold weather the cabin was heated. There was also open seating in the bows and baggage accommodation under the bow and

LANCASTER CANAL.

NOTICE IS HEREBY GIVEN, that the Canal from Lancaster to Kendal is intended to be opened for general Trade, on FRIDAY, the 18th day of June, 1819 *(not on Thursday, the 17th, as was previously advertized)*; and that PACKET BOATS will be established, for the conveyance of Passengers and Parcels, between Lancaster and Kendal. to set out every Morning *(Sundays excepted)* at 8 o'clock.

Advertisement for the packet boat service, Kendal Advertiser & Chronicle.
Kendal Public Library

stern decks. Passengers could have first or second-class cabins and refreshments on board. In winter an iceboat pulled by eleven horses kept the canal from freezing.

Boats left Kendal at six in the morning and arrived at Preston at one to connect with coaches to Manchester and Liverpool. For the return journey they left Preston at half past one and arrived in Kendal at a quarter to nine. To maintain their speed the packet boats were given right of way at all times, including priority at locks and bridges. Initially the boats travelled at only four miles an hour but in 1833 the 'Water Witch', drawn by horses at over eight miles an hour, became competitive with the mail coaches, the fastest of which could travel at only ten miles an hour.

Between July and December 1833 the Water Witch carried 16,000 passengers (19). The boats were pulled by pairs of horses changed every four miles and several of the stables built to house them, including those at Farleton, can be seen today along the line of the canal. The canal company boasted that *'for safety, economy and comfort no other mode of conveyance could be so eligible for them, - the timid might be at ease and the most delicate mind without fear.'*

The ride, amid the glorious countryside of what was formerly south Westmorland and North Lancashire, was so smooth and comfortable that it was preferred to coach travel on the improved turnpike roads. Standards of comfort ranged from carpeted luxury with piped central heating in the first class cabins to bare benches and plain wooden floors in the second class. One traveller, John Fox, noted in his diary for 1831 that the run from Preston to Kendal on the Lancaster Canal was *'the most delightful journey that I ever made in my life.'*

When the railway reached Preston there was a temporary increase in passenger traffic from Kendal, a new boat, 'The Crewdson', providing a service connecting with the North Union Train. William Dilworth Crewdson, a leading banker, was the chairman of the Kendal Canal Committee.

Packet boats operated until shortly after the coming of the railway to Kendal, the 1849 Directory announcing *'Fly Boats to Lancaster, Preston, etc from Canal Wharf, several times a week'*. However when, in 1886, Kendal Chamber of Commerce asked for steam passenger

Handbill advertising the packet boat service, March 1833

boats between Kendal and Farleton, the canal company declined (Public Record Office).

The destinations of 'carriers by water' from the Canal Warehouse listed in the 1829 Directory were:

Canal Packet Boats

BETWEEN

Kendal, Lancaster, & Preston.

THE NEW

SWIFT BOAT,

CALLED

" The WATER WITCH "

WILL be employed between LANCASTER and PRESTON, for the present, and perform the distance of 30 Miles in about three hours.

THE BOATS WILL SAIL

On MONDAY the 1st April,

From *Kendal* to *Preston*, and from *Preston* to *Kendal*, on alternate days, (Sundays excepted.)

The Packet will leave KENDAL at SIX o'Clock in the Morning, and LANCASTER at ONE o'Clock, every MONDAY, WEDNESDAY, and FRIDAY, and arrive at PRESTON soon after FOUR o'Clock,

And will leave PRESTON *at half after* NINE o'Clock, and LANCASTER at ONE o'Clock, every TUESDAY, THURSDAY, and SATURDAY, and arrive at KENDAL, at half-past SEVEN o'Clock.

FARES.

FIRST CABIN.—The whole length — — — — — Six Shillings;
Between *Kendal* and *Lancaster,* or *Lancaster* and *Preston,* Three Shillings;
shorter distances, *three half-pence* per Mile; but no Fare less than Nine Pence.

SECOND CABIN.—The whole length — — — — Four Shillings;
Between *Kendal* and *Lancaster,* or *Lancaster* and *Preston,* Two Shillings;
shorter distances, *one penny* per Mile; but no Fare less than Six Pence.

☞ *The Boat will sail from Kendal an hour earlier than heretofore, and both boats will leave Lancaster at ONE o'clock.*

*** Small Parcels between *Lancaster* and *Preston*, or *Lancaster* and *Kendal*, Six Pence each, the whole length between *Preston* and *Kendal*, One Shilling each, delivered free of Porterage,

Lancaster, March 28th, 1833.

C. CLARK, PRINTER, MARKET-PLACE, LANCASTER.

Handbill advertising the packet boat service, July 1833

James Machell to London, Liverpool, Manchester, Preston and Lancaster, and all parts of the south and to Wales, by Canal Boats. Sun. Tues. Thurs. & Fri. depart 3 mng. Arrive Sat. Mon. Tues. Thurs. Simon Myerscough, agent.

John Hargeaves – by Canal Boats to London, Liverpool, Manchester, Preston and Lancaster, and all parts of the south and to Wales, by Canal Boats Sunday, Tuesday, Thursday, and Friday dep. 3 mng. Arr. Saturday, Monday, Wednesday and Thursday 7 evng. Richard Walker, agent.

James Widner's vessels the Thomas, William and Dee convey goods from Hest Bank to Liverpool. Thomas Fisher, agent.

At the time of the 1841 population census there were three barges in the canal basin, two of the bargemen with wives and families on board.

Harris Museum & Art Gallery.

The Baines family of Preston in their Sunday best.

The packet boat Water Witch II, built in 1839, 76 feet long by 5 feet 11 inches in the beam, was used as an inspection boat for many years before being broken up. Photograph c.1880-1915.   *Courtesy of Lancaster Maritime Museum*

A report in the Westmorland Gazette of 18th June, 1887 gives an indication of the wages of the boatmen.

> *'The strike of canal boatmen over reducing the rate for conveying coal from Preston to Kendal from 1s to 11d per mile is over. Less than twenty years ago it was 9d and was gradually increased to 1s, remaining stationary at that rate for about twelve years. The men were earning about £1 10s 6d per week (after deducting the expense of providing the horse) and the new rate reduces their earnings by about 3s 10d per week. The strike ended during the week ending 16th June with the men accepting the new rate as it was clear that the employers would not budge.'*

A swift packet boat on the Forth and Clyde canal

Chapter Six

CASTLE MILLS TO PARR STREET

THE EARLY MILLS

Believed to have been originally the site of Kendal Castle's corn mill, this complex of mills later served many purposes, milling snuff, leather and hemp and 'friezing' or raising the nap on woollen cloth. Three 13th century documents refer to it as a fulling mill, fulling being the process of pounding cloth in a soap solution to strengthen it by shrinkage. A document of 1274 refers to both a water mill and a fulling mill in the lands of Kendal Castle.

In 1409 it is described as a *'water-corn-mill situate next the great park and a tenement next to the said mill.'* Corn milling is also indicated by records of tithes paid by the castle estates as *'tithe meal silver'* in 1459 and again in 1556 when it was recorded as *'belonging to the parsonage of Kendal.'*

In the later 18th century the Corporation owned the site and leased it to William Braithwaite and Isaac Wilson, shearman-dyers of Stramongate. Todd's map of 1787 shows a complex of buildings, outbuildings, weirs and bridges on the site. In 1805/6 this was completely rebuilt thirty or forty yards upstream as a woollen mill together with a new weir. Corn milling then ceased. At that date these were the only buildings on the east side of the river between the brewery on Stramongate and Nether Bridge.

Some difficulty was experienced in constructing the new bucket waterwheels for the mill, partly arising from the difficulty in transporting heavy goods to Kendal before the canal was built. The

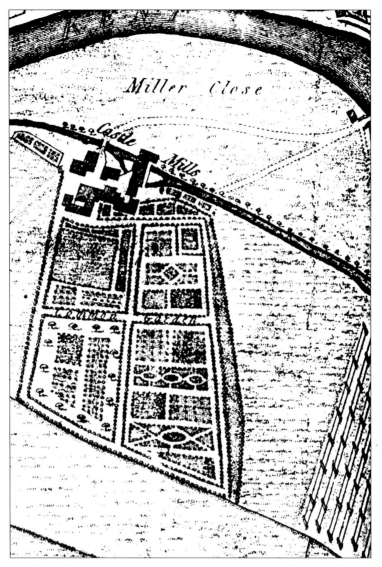

Castle Mills. *Todd's map of 1787*

castings, manufactured in Worcester, were carted to Liverpool, shipped to Milnthorpe and then carted to Kendal. Not surprisingly some components, *'got small pieces broken out of them: out of carelessness of the carter that carried them to the vessel.'* More seriously there were misunderstandings about the dimensions of the water wheel shafts required, a year and eight months elapsing between the placing of the original order and the final agreement over the price being reached by both parties (20).

J J & W WILSON'S MILLS

In 1840, the lease-holders changed the name of the company to J J & W Wilson. The population census returns for 1841, twenty-two years after the mill was completed, show twenty-three people living in the complex. Besides the manager there were two machine makers, a millwright, a joiner, two woollen spinners and a horn comb maker. George Riddle, forty, described himself as '*a walk miller*', a term derived from the medieval method of trampling woollen cloth in a vat of soap solution to shrink and strengthen it. By 1841 the process would have been carried out by fulling stocks operated by waterpower.

There appear to have been five households on the premises in 1841, the row of cottages next to Castle Lodge and the cottage in the Common Garden providing some but not all the accommodation needed. Allen Simpson, '*Woollener*' or woollen manufacturer and his family lived at Castle Lodge. In 1844 a shed mill was built, and in 1850 supplementary steam power was introduced, power-looms then beginning to replace handlooms. The company at this date produced

Mill girls at Castle Mills. *Margaret Duff Collection*

travelling rugs for railway passengers, tweeds, linings, collar checks and blankets, and at the Great Exhibition of 1851 took prizes for its rugs.

In 1854 the Corporation sold the mills to J. J. & W. Wilson who immediately began building the present mills for manufacturing rugs, tweeds, linings, horse cloths, horse collar checks and girth webs. They built a new thirty-horse power water wheel, about sixteen feet wide and fourteen feet diameter and, to ensure a power supply when the river was low, introduced in 1855 a thirty-horse power beam engine with an eighteen-foot diameter flywheel. In celebration of the opening of the new mills an entertainment was provided for the workforce in the upper storey of the west front, a room one hundred and eighty feet long and twenty-four feet wide, intended as a drying store. Speaking of modern developments in the industry, Mr J J Wilson compared hand spinning with machine spinning with which one man could spin three hundred threads. Besides the extension of the carpet trade in Kendal he referred to their own new products, trouserings and doeskin, a closely cut thick-twilled cloth (21).

The mill was highly mechanised, the wool, mostly imported, being cleansed and shredded mechanically before entering the carding machines and the fifteen hundred spindles of the spinning mules. After dyeing in the dye-house, the yarn was dewatered by a spinning process, dried and passed to the warping mill to be woven on power looms with weft from the weft-winding machines. The spinning and weaving sheds alone occupied two thousand, three hundred and fifty square yards and the firm employed some five hundred people.

Large extensions were made to the mills in 1872-74 and turbines were introduced in 1899. Water power continued in use however until after World War II. In 1933 J J & W Wilson went into liquidation and in 1933 the mills were bought by Messrs Goodacre for the production of Axminster Carpets (22).

One of the original four-storey buildings built by J J & W Wilson was unsuitable for carpet manufacturing and after a period when it was leased to one of the last horse-blanket manufacturers in town (Wilkinson's) was pulled down to make way for a new dye house. The original watercourse ran through the middle of the yard and was crossed by a bridge. The millrace was filled in in the late 1960s and all that remains now is a settling pond used for fire-fighting purposes. The

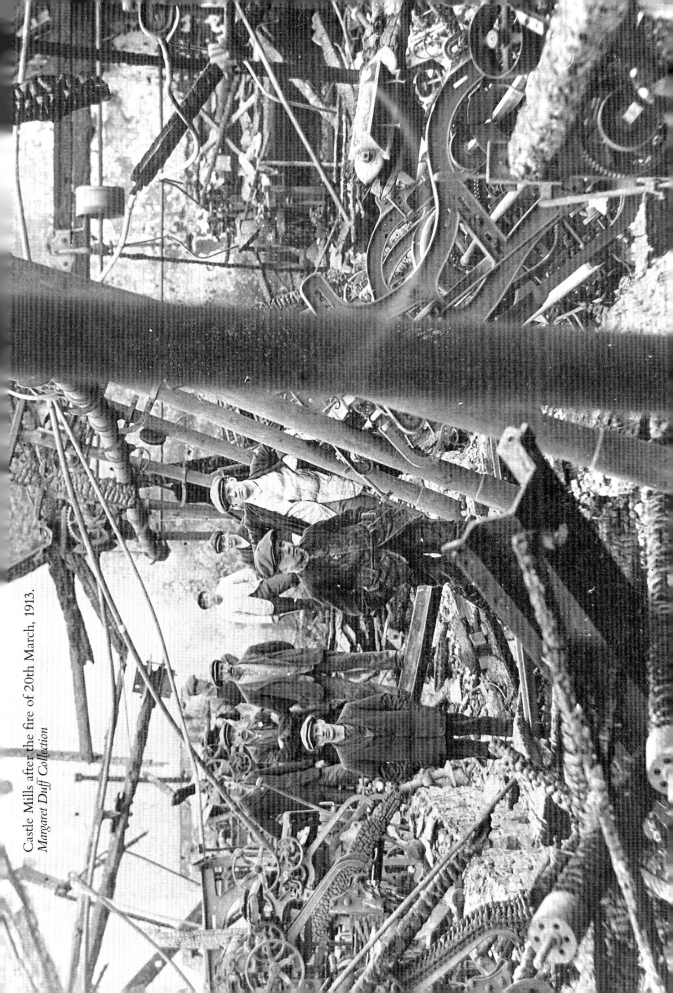

Castle Mills after the fire of 20th March, 1913.
Margaret Duff Collection

gatehouse that originally opened directly onto Aynam Road was replaced in a different position when one-way traffic was introduced to the town.

Of the surviving buildings, the main block comprises a central arched entrance built in deeply fissured limestone blocks in a rusticated style and two symmetrical wings, also in limestone but differently dressed. The arched entrance is perhaps part of the original 1806 building and the wings part of the 1854/55 reconstructions. The fissuring of the limestone of the arched entrance suggests that the stone was taken from a surface exposure of the Urswick beds which outcrop in Serpentine Woods. The stone for the 1854 extension was probably also from Kendal Fell but from the Dalton beds which have been quarried from the vicinity of the outcrop known locally as 'the Battleship'.

The engine house on the end of the building has two long windows and is in considerable disrepair. It is dated 1854.

Castle Mills. Main west front

Engine House with 1854 datestone

Detail of butt joint between 1806 entrance and 1854 extension

Margaret Duff Collection

Castle Mills. The tail-race, about 1900.

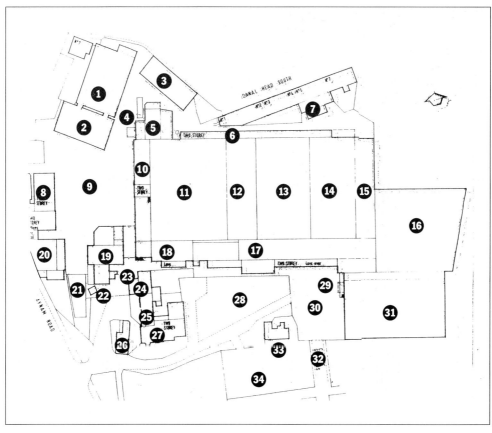

Messrs Goodacre's premises. J. Wilson, 1989

KEY TO MAP

1. Dye House
2. Dye House
3. Dye House
4. Tanks
5. Boiler House
6. Locker Rooms
7. Stores
8. Canteen
9. Open Yard
10. Dyed Yarn Store
11. No 1 Shed
12. No 2 Shed
13. No 3 Shed
14. No 4 Shed
15. No 5 Shed
16. Warehouse
17. Finishing
18. Bagging Shed
19. Workshops
20. Showroom
21. Resevoir
22. Pump House
23. Gate House
24. Stables
25. Cottage No 5
26. Cottage No 6
27. Offices
28. Garden
29. Loading Bank
30. Open Yard
31. Despatch
32. Castle Gardens
33. Castle Garden Cottage
34. Car Park

CASTLE LODGE

A 1782 sale notice in the Cumberland Pacquet records this house as an inn with a brew house, seed shop, stable, and hayloft. It was set in the Common Garden, a freehold property of nearly five acres with '*a variety of choice Fruit Trees*' and '*a Flower Garden, or Nursery, and Hot Beds, and a great many beautiful Walks and Arbors laid out in Taste*'. It was advertised to let two years later as '*all that Common Garden, consisting of four acres, bowling green and dwelling house now and for many years past a public house*'. The bowling green and '*walks laid out in taste*' are well illustrated in Todd's map of Kendal of 1787 (see page 60). Castle Lodge, was occupied in 1910 by Frederick Park, an electro plater, and the gardener's cottage, No 5 Castle Mills, was occupied by a Thomas Dalziell, described as a porter in the Castle Lodge laundry. Three other cottages, Nos 2 and 10 Castle Mills and Castle Mill Foot were also occupied as dwellings in 1910, the latter by Robert Williams, a miller. The end cottage behind the present gatehouse had a bakery at the back where oatcakes were sold.

Until recently a dwelling, the house has an attractive 18th century elevation facing east across the former 'Common Garden'. Apart from a Victorian addition at its south western corner it appears to be as shown on Todd's map of 1787. It has a walled garden abutting its east side, with

Castle Lodge

Cottages adjacent to Castle Lodge

an arched gateway and a terrace of mill cottages enclosing its west side, also apparently of 18th century date. There are a few ancient Yew trees near the entrance to the mill yard; one damaged gate pillar has survived at the former entrance to Castle Lodge; and a stone-built gardener's cottage is occupied as a dwelling.

PARR STREET BRIDGE

Beyond Castle Mills the canal continued south to pass under Parr Street at Parr Street Bridge. Built in 1818-19 it served adequately until about 1888 when it was widened to allow houses to be built on what is now Sunnyside. The parapets were taken down and a row of girders placed across the road extending beyond the bridge on the northern side. Arched brickwork was constructed between the girders and iron plates riveted onto them, providing a base for new parapet walls. Decorative strips were fixed to the plates to give a panelled effect and a new flight of steps was built at the south-east corner to give access to the towpath to Sunnyside. The bridge shows well from its underside the method used to widen it.

A news item of 5th May 1888 (Westmorland Gazette) reported that:

> *'The two iron girders for the new part of the bridge across the canal leading to Castle Fields (Parr Street) arrived by road yesterday afternoon. They weighed about eleven tons and were carted to the canal basin whence they were floated to the bridge.'*

Parr Street Bridge from the North

Details of the underside of the bridge showing the method of widening it

Steps giving access to Sunnyside. Note the iron ties between the parapet capping stones

MAP OF THE HISTORIC BUILDINGS
NETHER STREET TO GARDEN ROAD

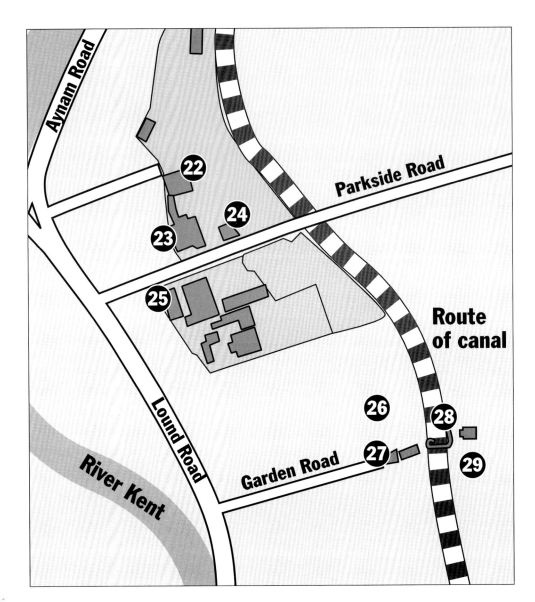

KEY TO MAP

22. Former Gasworks Building
23. Former Gasworks Offices
24. Former Gasworks Gatehouse
25. Electricity Undertaking
26. Lound Wharf
27. Ivy Bank and Cottages
28. Change Bridge and Horse Ramps
29. Cinder Ovens Field

Chapter Seven

THE LOUND WHARVES AND THEIR ASSOCIATED INDUSTRIES

THE GAS WORKS

In Carlisle, with coal available at a distance of about twenty miles, gas lighting was used from 1819 onwards not only for streets but for shops, factories and some private houses. Kendal, where coal was not easily got until the canal was open, had to wait until 1826 for a similar service (19).

The need to light the town had been recognised by the Kendal Fell Act of 1767 and prior to 1826 about one hundred and forty whale oil lamps had been provided to light the streets. The town was nevertheless so dark that in 1817 the Westmorland Advertiser (5th July) reported that a gang of youths nightly paraded the streets and when the watch had passed extorted drink or money from citizens.

Kendal's Gas Works were completed by the Kendal Fell Trust, as the 'Kendal Gas Light and Coke Company,' in 1825 and by 1860 one hundred and thirty-two street gas lights were functioning. At first domestic gas was regarded with some scepticism, the current joke referring to 'taking a candle to see if the gas was alight!' (12). When Queen Victoria was crowned in 1838 it was still a novelty and the Mayoral Dinner in the Kings Arms featured:

> *'an ingenious device of a gas pipe in the shape of a crown placed behind theMayor's chair. It was not observed, except by those who were near and*

when, by the application of a candle, it started as if by magic, into splendour, with its countless little jets, the effect was very striking'(12).

A balloon ascent from the gas works attracted much publicity in 1825. The gas works initially had two gasholders, one in reserve in case of accident, together containing twenty-two thousand cubic feet of gas. It had fourteen retorts heated by two ovens, said to have yielded coke equal to that produced by cinder ovens. The enterprise became the Kendal Union Gas and Water Company in 1849. Hoggarth's map of 1853, compared with John Wood's map of 1833,

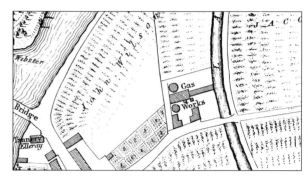

Gas Works 1833. John Wood's map of Kendal

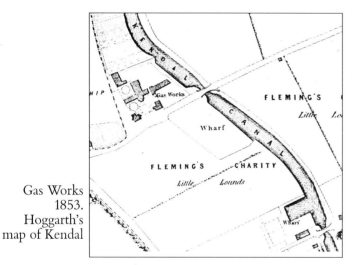

Gas Works 1853. Hoggarth's map of Kendal

shows two additional buildings, a northern wing added to the main E-W Block of buildings and a new building in the north-western corner of the site.

Four buildings of note in this complex survive. A large building with a three arched entrance facing east at ground level and three arched windows with modern sashes above is constructed of random stone between corners of dressed quoins and could be of 1833-1853 date.

On the east side of the entrance from Parkside Road is a building of hand sawn limestone blocks with three incongruously modern

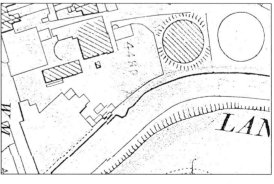

Gas Works 1912. District Valuer's map

windows on each of two floors and a pair of pilasters with capitals on either end of the roadside elevation. It appears to be part of the original 1825 Gas Light and Coke Company's buildings.

On the west side are what appear to be the original entrance gateposts with replacement caps and, west of the gateway, a building with a 1902 date stone believed to have been designed by Joseph Bintley, the Borough architect at that date.

Little of the Gas Works now survives apart from the main store, the joiners' and blacksmiths' workshops and the offices, much altered, either side of the gate onto Parkside Road, formerly Gas House Lane.

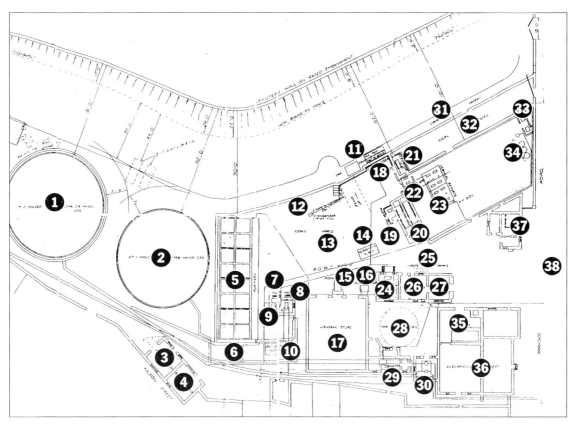

Gas Works 1960.   *Ian Murray, Norweb*
Key: 1. No 2 Holder, Coal or Mixed Gas; 2. No 1 Holder, Carbonated Water Gas; 3. Joiners' Shop; 4. Blacksmiths' Shop; 5. Purifiers 6. Oxide Pit; 7. Meter House; 8. Coal Gas; 9. C W Gas; 10. Benzole Plant; 11. Tar Tank; 12. Condenser Water Well; 13. Coke Yard; 14. Screening Plant; 15. Rotary Washer; 16. Livesey Washer; 17. General Store; 18. Condenser; 19. Pump House; 20. Boilers; 21. Elevator Engine; 22. Extractor Engine; 23. Vertical Retorts; 24. Exhausts; 25. Waste Liquor Tanks; 26. S/A Plant; 27. S/A Store; 28. Tar and Liquor Well; 29. Booster; 30. Governors; 31. Canal Wharf; 32. Coal Store; 33. Blower; 34. C W G Plant; 35. Boiler; 36. Electricity Department; 37. Offices; 38. Parkside Road.

However, one interesting feature has been relocated to the entrance of Abbot Hall – the façade of Francis Webster's original 1825 Meter House. Inscribed over its doorway is the phrase: '*Ex fumo dare lucem*', translating roughly as 'from smoke let light break out'. It is a quotation from '*Ars Poetica*' (Art of Poetry), a book by the Roman poet Horace, written about 30 BC. It referred originally to poetic inspiration (23).

Another surviving fragment of the Corporation Gas Works is the plaque from a demolished gasholder, now in a private garden in Aynam Place. It records the erection of the gasholder in 1901 by Clayton Son and Company Limited, contractors of Hunslet, Leeds.

The District Valuer's map, partially revised in 1912, shows the 1825 Meter House and the building in the northwest corner of the site but there are many additions and alterations from

Screening plant 1960.   *John Marsh Collection*

Parkside Road Bridge and the Gas Works prior to demolition.   *Margaret Duff Collection*

Workmen at Kendal Gas Works. *Margaret Duff Collection*

Former Gas Works building north of the Parkside Road entrance

earlier layouts, including new gasholders. The building on the southwest corner of the site with a 1902 datestone housed the Electricity Department.

The relocated Meter House façade

Wrought-iron gates, Parkside Road entrance.   *Courtesy Ian Murray, Norweb*

Gas holder, Aynam Road

The canal as seen from Gas Works Bridge. The end of the wharf projecting into the canal is shown on Hoggarth's map of 1853. *Trevor Hughes Collection*

Gas Works Bridge, Parkside Road in 1854.
Margaret Duff Collection

THE ELECTRICITY UNDERTAKING

On the south side of Parkside Road, opposite the 1902 Electricity building, the 1912 map (see page 74) shows a building and yard described in the District Valuer's ledger as 'Kendal Urban District Council Engine Shed and Yard'. The engine shed housed the generator of the Kendal Electricity Undertaking set up in the 1880s.

1902 electricity building west of the Gas Works entrance

Former engine shed, Parkside Road

THE THREE WHARVES IN LITTLE LOUND

The name 'The Lound', formerly meaning a small wood or glade (24), is generally understood to mean the highway south from the south-east end of Nether Bridge. However on the first Ordnance Survey map of 1858 it is printed horizontally across the area between the road and the canal. Little Lound is shown on Hoggarth's map of 1853 as the block of land between what is now Parkside Road and Lound Street.

In the Canal Committee's minutes for 1st June 1818 is a report that *'It is necessary to wall the three wharves in Little Lound as soon as possible,'* and a minute of their meeting a week later records that, *'The construction of the three wharves had been let to Messrs Carradus for the sume of 6s 6d per superficial perpendicular yard.'* The work was completed by October and the wharves were advertised to let but in November 1819 another minute records that, *'Three wharves in the Canal Basin are yet unoccupied and three also at the Little Lound.'*

The most northerly of the Little Lound wharves appears to have been on the north side of Parkside Road on the west bank of the canal, adjacent to the Gas Works. The second wharf was also on the west bank of the canal, immediately south of Parkside Road and denoted 'Timber Wharf' on the 1858 Ordnance Survey map.

The third wharf was also on the canal's west bank on the north side of Change Bridge and is shown on the 1858 Ordnance Survey map as 'Lound Wharf', subscripted 'Coal Depot.' A heap of stored coal or coke can be seen in the depot illustrated on p 111. The exit from this wharf

---

WHARFS AT THE CANAL BASIN, KENDAL.

TO BE LET BY PRIVATE CONTRACT,
To be entered on as soon as the Canal is open,
THREE WHARFS, situate at the south end of the town adjoining to the Canal, in a field called Little Lound, about one hundred yards from Nether Bridge.
For particulars apply to Mr. Alderman T. HARRISON, Lowther-street, Kendal.
Kendal, October 14, 1818.

Advertisement in the Westmorland Gazette and Kendal Advertiser

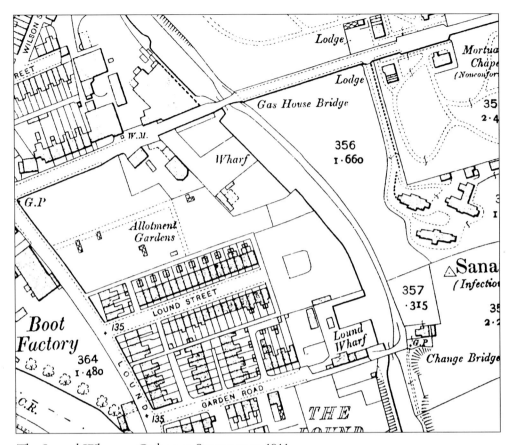

The Lound Wharves. Ordnance Survey map 1911

on to what is now Garden Road was only yards away from the rear entrance to the Lound Iron Foundry which no doubt used it for transporting iron and iron goods via the canal.

Coal deliveries to the Gas Works via the canal continued for almost another century, the population census for 1881 showing a canal boat, the 'Kenneth' moored at the Lound Wharf. On board were the 47 year old 'captain', Daniel Ashcroft of Preston; his 49 year old wife Elizabeth and his 19 year old daughter Elizabeth, both also of Preston; the 'mate' 24 year old Elijah Norman of Lancaster; and a visitor, Elizabeth Tickell of Preston.

South of Parkside Road, the filled-in canal retains its curving eastern boundary line in the frontage of the new industrial buildings. Immediately south of the K Village overflow car park some of the coping stones of the former Lound Wharf are visible on its north and west sides.

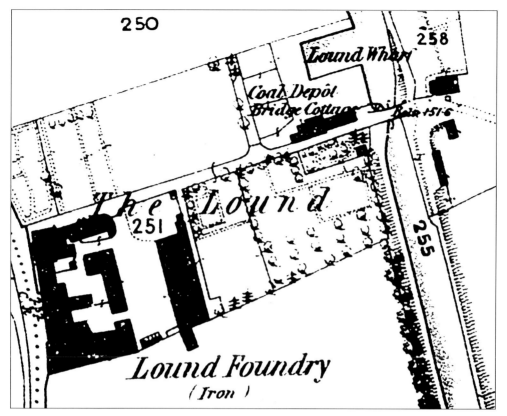

Lound Wharf, Coal Depot and Lound Foundry. Ordnance Survey map 1858

THE LOUND FOUNDRY

A plan signed by Henry Hoggarth and dated 1845 (25) shows the Lound Foundry as 'measured for John Wakefield Esquire being purchased by Mr Stephenson and Company for Mr Watson.' Lound Street was not then built but the Kendal-Burton Road is shown connected to Change Bridge by a right-of-way fourteen and a half feet wide. The foundry stood in a four acre site extending either side of this right-of-way just north of the Lound Wharf. The importance of the wharf to the operation of the foundry is indicated by a notice in the Westmorland Gazette of January 29th, 1848 advertising the foundry as to let:

> *The establishment has been fitted up within the last three years, and the machinery and tools are all of the best make, and in capital working condition. The foundry has three cupolas and four powerful cranes, and is well calculated for casting up to fourteen tons. The fitting-up shop has six double-geared hand and slide lathes, drilling, boring, screwing and slotting*

Coping stones of the north side of the Lound Coal Wharf remaining above the infill

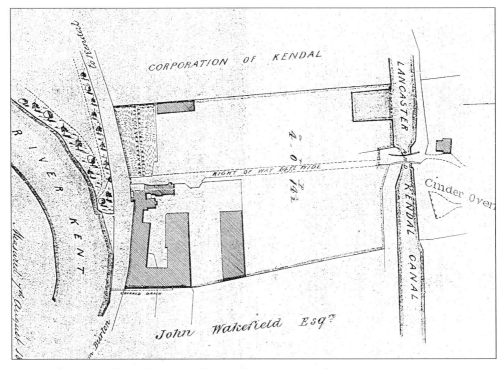

Hoggarth's 1845 plan of the Lound Foundry

*machines, all on the best modern principle; and the smithy has a full
complement of excellent tools for twenty-five hearths.*

*The premises are situated in the healthy town of Kendal, on the banks of
the Lancaster Canal, with which they communicate by a private basin,
furnished with cranes for landing or shipping any weight. They also front
the High Road from Lancaster to Kendal and are near the Lancaster and
Carlisle Railway; thus having cheap and ready communication with all
parts of the Kingdom.'*

Clearly the foundry had a considerable capacity for large castings and it
seems likely that it was equipped to cast girders for bridges on the
Lancaster and Carlisle Railway and the Kendal and Windermere
Railway, both of which opened in 1846.

According to its letterhead, Day's Foundry moved to the Lound in
1850 when Elizabeth Winder occupied it. Evidently the sale to Mr
Watson fell through as in 1848 the property was purchased from John
Wakefield by the Websters' partner Miles Thompson, as stated in his
will of 1866. The foundry on this site closed in 1893 when it moved to
Canal Head (1).

Change Bridge. The western horse ramp before restoration.

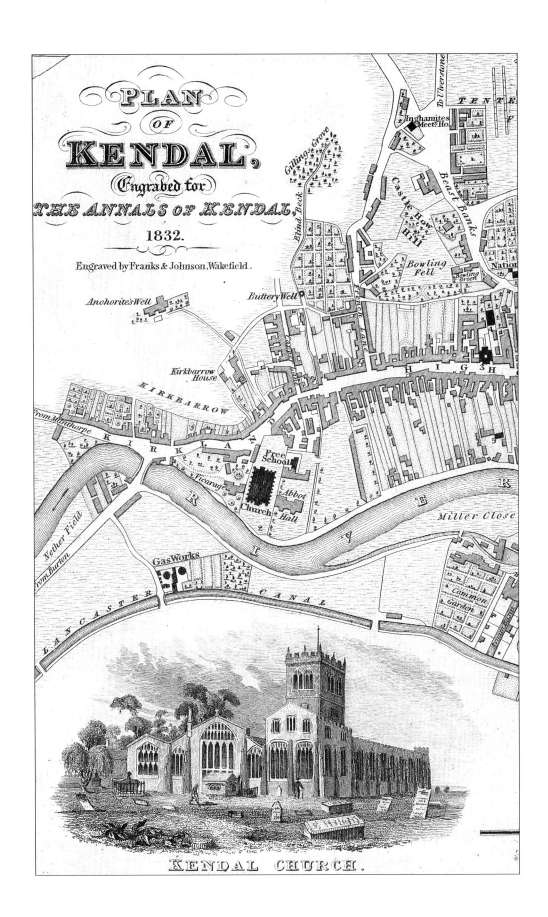

PLAN
OF
KENDAL,
Engraved for
THE ANNALS OF KENDAL,
1832.

Engraved by Franks & Johnson, Wakefield.

KENDAL CHURCH.

Chapter Eight

CHANGE BRIDGE, IVY BANK AND THE CINDER FIELD

CHANGE BRIDGE

Hoggarth's plan of 1853 shows three coal storage bays west of Lound Wharf and a new building on the north side of the right-of-way adjacent to Change Bridge, the whole property in the possession of Miles Thompson who at this date had become a partner in the Websters' architectural practice.

Miles Thompson, 1800 - 1872, joined the Websters as a draughtsman in the 1820s, becoming a partner in 1845 and carrying on the business after George Webster's death in in 1864. In 1842 he bought from his father John Thompson the site of what is now Nos 14-16 Collin Croft and the land behind it up to Beast Banks.

Change Bridge from the north.

Change Bridge   *British Waterways*

Change Bridge. North side. Tree damage to parapet

On Beast Banks he built a terrace of cottages, one for his brother Robert and one for his own occupation. For Robert he also built the warehouse, now converted to dwellings, with the Italianate arch and triple window above it spanning the steps leading up to Beast Banks.

Miles was subsequently the architect of various prominent Kendal buildings including the former washhouse and baths, now Shearman House; the Kirkland Schools; and a new house for himself beside the canal at Change Bridge.

South of Change Bridge the towpath was on the west of the canal but, to avoid interference with loading and unloading of barges moored at the wharves, the towpath continued north from the bridge to Canal Head only on the eastern side. At Change Bridge barge horses on the west bank were led up a ramp and over the bridge to continue on the other side. Barges travelling south followed the reverse procedure.

This charming piece of canal architecture was rapidly deteriorating until recently under the pressures of vandalism and neglect. Trees had pushed out the retaining walls of the horse ramps on both sides of the bridge and vandals had demolished a loosened section of the west ramp. There were visible cracks and fissures on the south side and frost damage from water penetration. Some of the coping stones had been

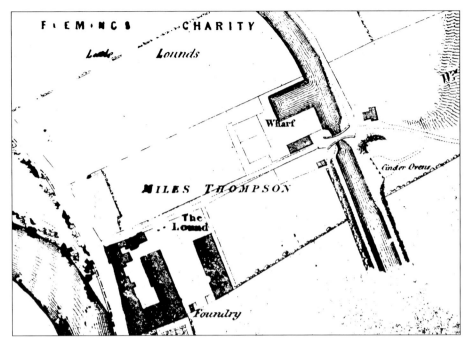

Hoggarth's 1853 map of Kendal, detail

pushed off the ramp walls and the whole structure needed urgent attention. At the time of writing, the bridge is under repair, funded by a Heritage Lottery grant to Kendal Civic Society and South Lakeland District Council.

IVY BANK

Hoggarth's 1853 map shows, immediately west of this ramp, a rectangular building which is still at least partially in existence. On its north side, facing the former coal wharf, the ground floor has a central stone arch wide enough to have admitted a cart for loading from or unloading into warehouse space on the floor above. There are matching pairs of doors/windows either side of the arch which suggest stables for work horses.

West of this building and overlapping it, significantly with an unbonded joint, is another building, far superior in quality of design and masonry work. Its southwest corner is chamfered back at ground floor level to avoid constricting the entrance to the wharf from Garden Road, and its main living accommodation was raised above the wharf level

Miles Thompson's house, west elevation

over semi-cellars (26). This was Miles Thompson's own house and shows features of his architectural style.

Probably at the same time as this house was built, as shown by the maps between 1845 and 1853, the south side of the old warehouse was converted to cottages or at least upgraded to present a better appearance adjacent to Miles Thompson's front door. The extent of his property in the Lound is indicated in his will of 1866 (27):

> *'I give and devise to my brother, Marcellus Thompson his heirs and assigns all those my Messuages Tenements or Dwelling Houses, Workshops, Yards, Sheds, Foundry, Gardens and other hereditaments which I purchased from the late John Wakefield Esquire deceased situate at the Lound aforesaid.'*

This Marcellus Thompson is listed in the 1869 and 1873 directories as a marble mason at Lound Works where in 1879 he also dealt in coal, flagstones, bricks, chimney pots and tiles and offered *'monumental designs on application'*.

The whole Ivy Bank property – house, cottages and former stables has recently undergone redevelopment as flats.

THE CINDER FIELD

Coke was first made by igniting heaps of coal covered with turves, as in charcoal burning, but by the late 1820s coke was already produced in Kendal incidentally to the production of gas. In the 1830s smelting technology had shown that although coal and coke yielded the same amount of melted iron for the same weight of fuel, the speed at which it was produced using coke was almost twice that using coal (28). Coke was therefore preferable since the capacity of a cupola (furnace) for large castings increased in proportion to the speed of melting.

Holme coke ovens.
Courtesy Cumbria County Council

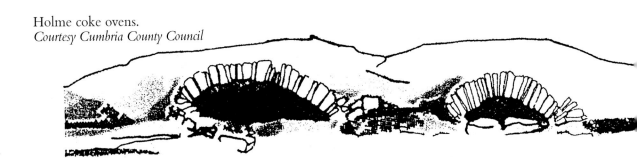

The Corn Rents map and schedule of 1836 show no cinder ovens on the field east of Change Bridge and describe it as *'used for hay.'* However the map signed by Henry Hoggarth and dated 1845 (Cumbria Record Office) shows a bank of five 'cinder ovens', their erection thus falling between these two dates. It seems likely that they were used to produce coke for the Lound Foundry, which as noted, was advertised in 1848 as having three cupolas.

Coke ovens were usually built in banks of three or more. A set of four would allow one to be being filled, one to be burning, one to be cooling down and one to be being emptied concurrently. An oven would be filled with coal and lit and the entrance would then be bricked up to restrict the air supply. The exhaust gases would escape through a small aperture left in the top of the oven. After about three days the bricks would be removed and any remaining fire extinguished. The oven would then be allowed to cool and its contents emptied.

Remains of cinder ovens on this site survived to within living memory, a local resident in his late eighties recently recalling that there was one large arched oven standing alone and three smaller ovens, and that the whole field was covered by cinders. The ovens can be readily identified on the 1858 Ordnance Survey map. The many large blocks of stone on the approach to the Cinder Field have no historical interest and were placed there recently to prevent travellers from occupying the site.

Cinder ovens further south along the canal are referred to in a handbill in the Crewdson Archive (29) which advertised the letting in December 1820 of two wharves at Crooklands *'in one of which the Canal Company will erect ovens for the burning of cinders, if required by taker.'* The wharf was said to be *'well situated for the sale of coal and cinders to a large neighbourhood requiring a considerable consumption of both articles.'*

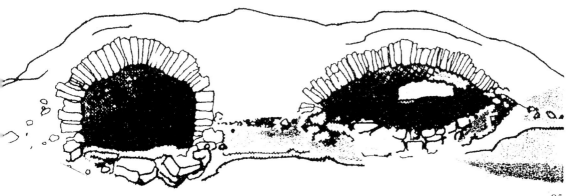

MAP OF THE HISTORIC BUILDINGS
LEISURE CENTRE TO HELME LODGE

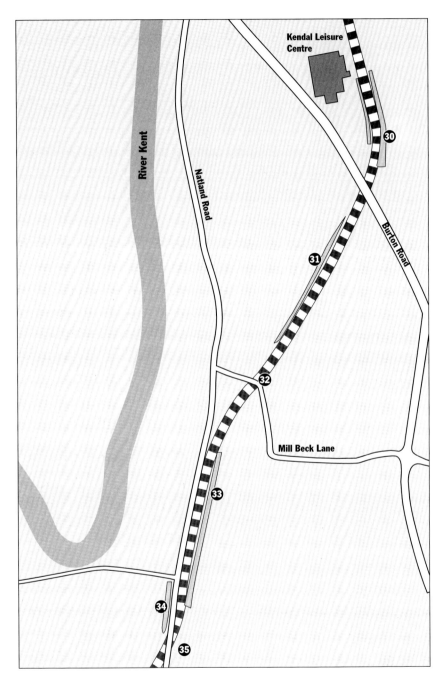

KEY TO MAP

30. Milestone
31. Wooded Embankments
32. Natland Mill Beck Lane Bridge

33. Avenue of Beeches
34. Ramp to former Natland
    Road Bridge
35. Gateway to Helme Lodge

Chapter Nine

SOUTH TO THE TOWN BOUNDARY

THE CANAL BANKS

At the rear of the Leisure Centre a low retaining wall begins where the canal passed through rising ground and defines the edge of the towpath. Both banks are well covered with self-generating native woodland probably originally planted to stabilize the banks. A little further south a row of mature beeches begins on the east bank and continues with some gaps to a point opposite the modern K Shoe factory buildings. Here they begin again and continue along the end of the Helme Lodge Park as far as its Burton Road entrance. The size of the trees suggests they were planted when the park was laid out, in about 1824 when Helme Lodge was built. An undated handbill, probably of the 1820s, threatens prosecution for people *'trespassing in the plantations.'* A boundary marker from the canal erected by the railway company south of Natland Mill Beck Bridge after it bought the canal in 1846, is in Lancaster Museum. Also at the rear of the Leisure Centre, just south of the overflow car park, at the foot of the eastern bank, a canal milestone has survived inscribed on the south side with the numerals 26, the distance in miles to Lancaster and, on the north side, 1, the distance to Kendal.

Planted beeches, west boundary of Helme Lodge Park

Canal milestone, 26 miles to Lancaster. Rear of
Leisure Centre

THE BRIDGES

The bridge carrying the Burton Road (A65) over the canal has been completely filled in and replaced by a modern road. The next bridge south over Natland Mill Beck Road appears to be totally original and the stones capping the edges of the canal are still visible. On the west side the masonry shows grooves cut by barge towropes where the towpath narrowed.

The bridge over Natland Road, which formerly carried the drive into Helme Lodge Park was removed in the 1960s when the stone was used to build 66 Sedbergh Road. The ramp leading up to it on the west side of the Burton Road remains however with part of its parapet.

Highgate Settlings, now replaced by the A65 road to Burton
Trevor Hughes Collection

Natland Mill Beck Lane Bridge

Steps from the towpath to Natland Mill Beck
Lane Bridge

Detail of Natland Mill Beck Road
Bridge, showing grooves worn by
tow-ropes

Western ramp of the former Natland Road Bridge

Gateway to Helme Lodge formerly approached from Natland Road Bridge

HELME LODGE

George Webster designed Helme Lodge in 1824 for Mr W. D. Crewdson, chairman of the Kendal Canal Committee (30). In addition to the bridge over the canal giving access to Helme Lodge Park he had adjacent to it a private landing stage from which he could board the fast packet boats south (31). A few hundred metres northwest of the Lodge, in a private garden on the west bank of the canal, was the Helme Lodge ice house, built in the corner formed by the canal and the bridge leading to Natland Mill Beck. Constructed of limestone, it was about fourteen feet deep, the top being corbelled in over a cylindrical chamber. A nearby resident recalled seeing ice being cut from the canal with a saw and thrown into the pit in about 1905 (32).

LOW MILLS

No direct evidence has come to light of the use made of the canal by these mills but as they operated as an iron foundry from 1826 to 1850 they probably used the canal for long distance heavy transport. The mills were used for many different purposes in the course of their history, a number of which are identified in the local directories thus:

Webster's design for Helme Lodge, 1824

1829   Thos. Winder & Sons, Iron Founders, Low Mills
1849   Thos. Winder & Sons, Iron Founders, Low Mills
1849   Caleb Metcalf & Sons, Woollen Mfrs
1885   Joseph Troughton & Sons, Comb Mfr., Low Mills
        John Ireland & Co., Mfrs. of Woollens, Linseys etc.
        John E Gawith, Snuff Mfr. (and at Lowther Street)
1894   John Ireland & Co., Woollen and Horse Clothing Mfrs.
1905   Richardson & Co., Woollen Mfrs. & Woollen Yarn Spinners

The mills are said to have been burned down in 1891.

HELSINGTON MILLS

Predecessors of the present mills are recorded in 1297, 1323 and 1581, but the great weir serving the present two mills is believed to have been built by Messrs. Webster and Holmes for their marble works in about 1800. The Gazette of 1829 described their operation thus:

'The late Mr Webster, Architect, constructed machinery on the River Kent for sawing and polishing marble. The surrounding mountainous district supplies the finest black, and other marble, and the advantage possessed by Kendal of sea and inland navigation facilitates the importation of Italian marble to be here manufactured and re-shipped to most of the principal towns in the Kingdom.'

The marble mill with its large head-race and wheel in the centre of the mill was taken over in 1895 by Messrs. Chaplow and for many years the wheel provided the power to drive and light Chaplow's Engineering Works. Gawith, Hoggarth took over the small mill with its undershot wheel at the west end and converted it into a snuff mill in 1822 (33).

The Helsington complex includes a weir on the River Kent, two mills and the head-races and tail-races serving them. The upper mill was formerly Gawith, Hoggarth's Snuff Mill, a two-storied building with an outside staircase and an undershot waterwheel in place. The mill downstream had a waterwheel in the centre of the building which was removed, a large window filling its place. The floor was concreted and for many years the building has been Chaplow's workshop.

Helsington Weir

Helsington Snuff Mill

Chaplow's workshop, formerly the smaller mill

Undershot waterwheel, Helsington Snuff Mill

Chapter Ten

RECREATION

Throughout its history, the canal has been put to a variety of recreational uses, many of them illicit. The handbill illustrated below threatens a month's hard labour in the House of Correction for anyone found fishing or bathing in the canal or *'hunting rats or other vermin upon the banks.'* Bathers were reproved in a Mrs Grundy-ish editorial in the

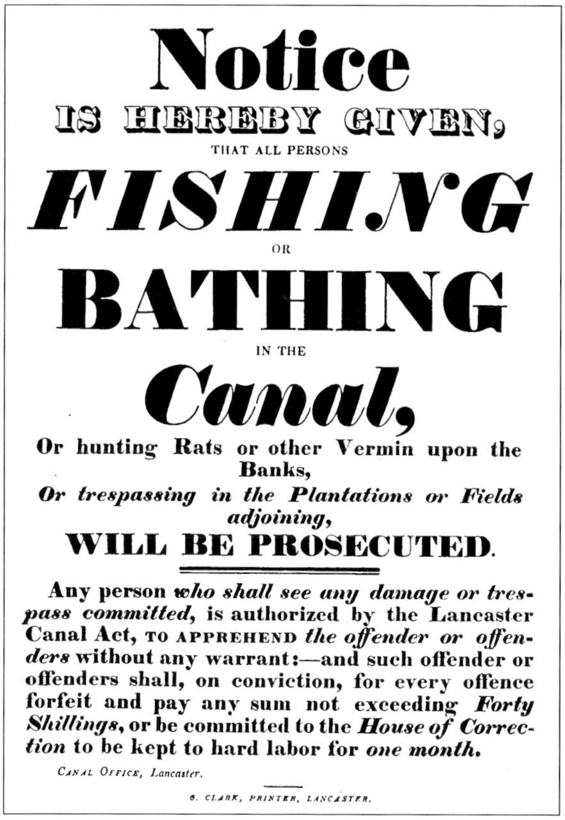

Notice
IS HEREBY GIVEN,
THAT ALL PERSONS

FISHING
OR

BATHING
IN THE

Canal,

Or hunting Rats or other Vermin upon the Banks,

Or trespassing in the Plantations or Fields adjoining,

WILL BE PROSECUTED.

Any person *who shall see any damage or trespass committed,* is authorized by the **Lancaster Canal Act, TO APPREHEND** *the offender or offenders* without any warrant:—and such offender or offenders shall, on conviction, for every offence forfeit and pay any sum not exceeding *Forty Shillings,* or be committed to the *House of Correction* to be kept to hard labor for *one month.*

CANAL OFFICE, Lancaster.

O. CLARK, PRINTER, LANCASTER.

19th century handbill(3)

Skating on the canal about 1900 *Margaret Duff Collection*

Westmorland Gazette in June 1839 condemning, '*The practice of a set of uncultivated fellows every evening (deciding) to strip on the canal banks near the town and wash their carcases without the least regard for decency. Consequently respectable females cannot get the benefit of their usual walk along the canal!*'

Skating on the canal was popular but frustrated by the ice-boats. The Westmorland Gazette in January 1887 reported:

> *The steam ice boat forced its way up the canal to Kendal on Thursday afternoon to the disgust of hundreds of skaters and sliders. A large crowd accompanied it from Hawes Bridge and dismal were the howls of disappointment as the boat crunched its way onwards. The heavy rain on Tuesday had smoothed the surface of the ice, and the frost, which followed on Tuesday night put the ice in excellent trim. The canal had been frozen for about five weeks, the ice averaging five inches thick.*'

The skaters response was to form the Kendal Skating Club which purchased Rinkfield, a field opposite Low Mills which could be flooded by opening a sluice gate from the canal. Members paid three shillings a year subscription and much of Kendal's youth learned to skate here in hard winters.

Kendal's May Day celebrations originally centred on the maypole which stood in Kirkland opposite the Wheat Sheaf until 1792 when it was removed as an obstruction to traffic. May Day celebrations nevertheless continued under the civilising influence of the evangelical movement, becoming more acceptable to Victorian taste. By the 1890s it had become regarded as a popular festival of Labour and as a treat for children with parades, sports and the crowning of the Queen of the May.

The photograph above shows the coal carts of the Wigan Coal and Iron Company drawn up on Little Aynam at the foot of Canal Head North for a May Day procession. The name on the carts of the Company's agent, Geo. B. Greenall, no doubt the man in the billycock hat, is given in an advertisement in Bulmer's trade directory of 1885.

KENDAL AGENCY.

Wigan Coal and Iron Company,
LIMITED,
GEORGE B. GREENALL,
Agent for Kendal and District North of, and including Carnforth.

YARDS AND OFFICES:—

| Railway Station, Windermere. | Canal Wharf, Crooklands. |
| Ditto, Milnthorpe. | Ditto, Tewitfield. |

And Canal Head, **KENDAL.**

Advertisement from Bulmer's trade directory of 1885

Zion Chapel Sunday School outing to Sedgwick   *Margaret Duff Collection*

School and Sunday school Whitsuntide outings on the canal barges to Levens Park were particularly popular. The Kendal author Theodora Wilson Wilson gives an account in 'T' Bacca Queen', published in 1901, which though set in a fictional narrative provides many interesting details. The event began with children and and adults assembling at a school on Fellside, possibly the National School built in 1818, the same year as the canal, and processing with flags and a band to Canal Head to arrive at 10.30. Four coal barges had been prepared with clean boarded decking, the sides lined with hessian and school forms provided for seating. Admission to the boat was by ticket, each boat holding 250 people old and young, with their provisions, hats, umbrellas, rugs and hymn books, all marshalled by the teachers and helpers wearing white rosettes. The horses, ribboned, braided and plaited with their brass-fitted parade harness brightly polished were hitched up and as soon as the vessels were under way the hymn singing began, at first spontaneously and then organised by the schoolteachers.

Arriving via a little lane from the canal down to Levens Park, the crowd settled in family groups under the trees, the children romping, skipping and racing while the teachers organised football, rounders and cricket, much of the afternoon being taken up with a match between older scholars versus teachers and juniors. Tea was organised by the gentry and approved helpers, with a sixteen-ounce spiced fruit bun distributed to each ticket holder and sweet tea, poured from stone jugs and replenished *ad libitum*. Organised races followed the tea, the Levens Hall party, with a carriage in attendance, having their own picnic tea before presenting the prizes.

This account provides a convincing sense of these canal outings in the early 1900s although the photograph of a Sunday-school outing to Sedgwick suggests a more conservative estimate of the passenger capacity of the barges.

The photograph below of three young men in a canoe, all smoking, shows a heap of coal in the background and appears to have been taken in the 1930s across the canal opposite the canal depot.

Boating on the canal beside the Coal Depot   *John Marsh Collection*

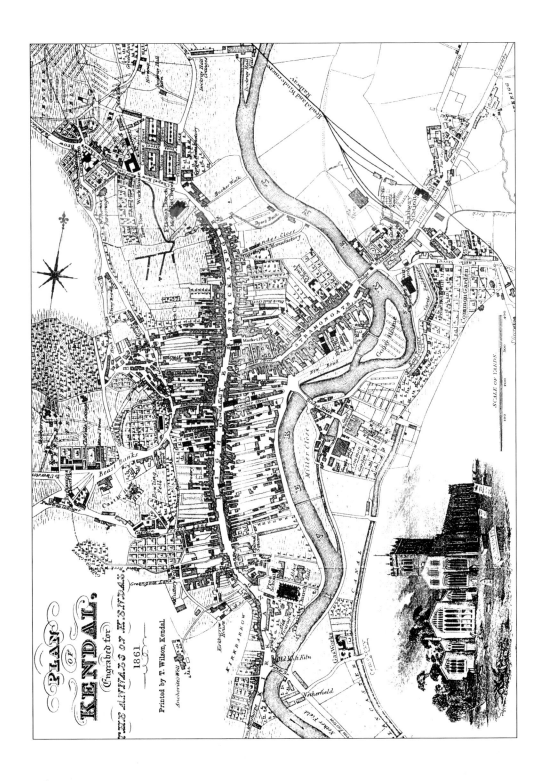

Chapter Eleven

EFFECTS OF THE CANAL
ON THE DEVELOPMENT
OF KENDAL

Kendal's population grew from about two thousand five hundred in the 1730s to about seven thousand five hundred in 1811, a threefold increase, which could only have been sustained by immigration (34). It would be difficult to analyse the effect of the canal on the town's demography but it seems more than a coincidence that the population continued to rise to nearly twelve thousand up to 1851, the period in which the canal reached its heyday before succumbing to the competition of the railway.

Prior to the coming of the canal, movement of merchandise in and out of the town was by packhorse or wagon. In the late 18th century, eight-horse wagons took twelve days for the round trip to London and back. Carriage was expensive, ninepence per ton per mile in 1771, a cost equivalent to about four hours of an artisan's work time (35). Although some coal was brought into Kendal from the Lancashire and Cumberland coalfields by packhorse, equally slow and expensive, the quantities were negligible.

The importance of bringing coal to Kendal was urged by Kendal Corporation almost a century before the arrival of the canal in a petition to the Treasury of 1729 for the remission of duty on coal. It claimed that, *'Kendal has been a place of great trade by the manufacture of several sorts of woollen stuff and tanning for leather, that turf (peat) hitherto their fuel being exhausted, the expense of firing has caused the utmost loss of trade.'* In 1807 an Act of Parliament was obtained empowering the Canal Company to build a tramway to Farleton so that limestone could be exported south after the coal barges had been emptied in Kendal. Once the canal was opened, coal was always the main cargo and supplies increased with the opening of the sea wharf close to the canal at Hest Bank and by the development of Glasson Dock at Lancaster. In 1826 a sixty-ton schooner, the 'Seaforth', sailed to Kendal with a cargo of salt from Northwich. General trade to Kendal on the canal increased from 194,000 tons in 1820 to 495,000 tons in 1830 (3).

The benefits to Kendal of the canal arose primarily from the low cost of transporting raw materials in and merchandise out of the town, two of the immediate effects of its arrival in 1819 being the reduction of the importance of Milnthorpe as a port and the displacement of the County's chief corn market from Burton-in-Kendal to Kendal itself. Infrastructure improvements incidental to constructing a good access to Canal Head also benefited the town's commerce. A newspaper cutting (36), undated but apparently from the late 1820s, gives an enthusiastic account of the benefits to the town:

'In noticing the other improvements of the town, amongst the most conspicuous and important are the Canal, and the immense pile of buildings adjoining its basin. These buildings have a two-fold importance in regard to this town; Firstly, as affording great facility to commerce; and secondly, because (being the property of the Corporation) they produce a large revenue per annum; a great part of which will probably be applied in making improvements in various parts of the town – they consist of two large warehouses and out-offices, one Hargreaves' and the other Widow Welch & Company, forming one handsome uniform building which for the convenience in the reception and forwarding of goods are not to be excelled in the Kingdom.

Webster's Marble Chimneypiece Manufactory. Fisher's Timber Yard and Workshops. Fawcett's Weighing Machine and House. Wilson & Company Dye House. A neat packet-house, at the head of the canal. Several dwellings, and offices attached to the different coal, slate, and timber wharfs. Kent Bridge a handsome and commodious structure, near where the old bridge stood; and the Mill-Race Bridge.

'The widening and improving the bottom of Lowther Street and Kent Street, with a large and extensive warehouse, and a handsome tier of buildings situate on the west side of it, present very considerable and beneficial changes; and the new erections and improvements in the principal streets, and other parts of the town, especially in the handsome appearance of many new shops, are too numerous to particularise.'

The 'Annals of Kendal' (14), published a few years later, described the effects of the canal on Kendal with equal enthusiasm:

'It discovered new channels of commerce – it brought that necessary commodity of manufactures, coal, at a cheaper rate; and exportation of our produce caused an increase of wealth, and an increase of the working population; and thus contributed, at once, all the means of commercial prosperity and public accommodation. We shall enumerate a few of the street improvements and additions, which immediately followed this event:

The old Miller Close Bridge, which had stood since 1743, and was very narrow, ill adapted to be the general medium of intercourse with the canal, was thrown down, and wholly rebuilt on a wider scale. The large warehouses, and other buildings at the canal harbour, were all erected at this time; Kent Lane (which before was very steep, and so narrow that two carts could scarcely pass) was thrown open, and the ascent considerably diminished; Long Pool was widened; Gandy Street erected; Kent Terrace and Castle Crescent were built shortly after. The Union Building Society commenced operations about this time; and indeed on every side, numerous habitations were added to the town. The National School reared its imposing front over the heads of the other buildings, and in a very short time, the town assumed a new modern appearance, so very different that any person having been absent a few years, could scarcely have identified it.'

This account might have included the widening of Stricklandgate and Wildman Street and the rebuilding of the bridge over Blindbeck to widen Kirkland, all in 1822. It fails to note however that the great Whig house–building programme of 1820, the 'Blue Buildings' of Caroline Street, Cross Street, Union Street and Strickland Place, was as much a consequence of Kendal's 1818 Parliamentary Election fever as of the opening of the canal.

Notwithstanding the availability of coal brought by the canal, Kendal was slow to convert from waterpower to steam power. The first steam engine in town was introduced in 1826 by Alderman Berry, at the end of what is now known as Berry's Yard, for cutting horn and ivory combs (37). However, steam power was not used for textile manufacture until 1843 when, according to the Westmorland Gazette, on the 4th of July, '*The leading manufacturers of the town assembled to witness the firing of the thirty horse power machine. This is the first time that the agency has been employed to supplement and assist the waterpower of the Kent.*' Three years later the Corporation had sold its interest in the Canal Company to the railway.

Subsidiary uses of the canal evolved as the years passed. In 1885 a line of six-inch pipes was laid to the locomotive shed at Oxenholme to convey water from the canal and in 1899 pipes were put in at Parr Street and Canal Head to flush the Kendal sewers periodically (Public Record Office).

Kendal from Thorny Hills. Painted by William Browne in 1819, the year the canal opened.

Chapter Twelve

THE TOWPATH WALK SOUTH — CANAL HEAD TO TEWITFIELD

The interested visitor who has explored the Canal Head and now proposes to follow the towpath south will see a number of interesting features, some industrial, some not, not so far mentioned in the text. At a walking rate of two miles an hour the walk from Canal Head to Tewitfield will take about seven and a half hours.

KENDAL CASTLE

The flight of steps from the towpath south of Parr Street Bridge gives access to the route up Sunnyside to the ruins of Kendal Castle, built mainly in the 13th century as the administrative centre of the Barony of Kendal, an area extending from Lunesdale to the lands of Furness. Crossing the moat at the northern entrance the visitor would once have passed through a gatehouse to the left of which the main structure is what remains of the manorial hall with its associated kitchens and undercrofts for storage. Opposite the hall at the south entrance is a small keep and a tower on the west seems to have given access to the top of the curtain wall. Below the turf are the remains of stables, a chapel, a dovecot and a well.

The castle was acquired by marriage by the Parr family in 1383, their youngest daughter, Kathryn Parr, becoming the last wife of Henry VIII. After the Parrs moved away from Kendal the castle fell into disrepair and has been a ruin since the late 16th century. It is now a Scheduled

Ancient Monument and has recently been consolidated with the help of a Heritage Lottery Grant. The castle is well provided with interpretative signs, its hilltop position providing commanding views up and down the valley of the River Kent and across the town of Kendal to the Lakeland Fells beyond.

Kendal Castle

THE SLEDDALL ALMSHOUSES

Lying between the towpath and the River Kent is Aynam Road, built in 1877 with, just south of Parr Street, a former organ works now converted to dwellings and a set of almshouses terminating in a Gothic chapel, now also divided into dwellings. The architect was Eli Cox and the almshouses were built in 1886 to commemorate Queen Victoria's Golden Jubilee of the following year. The benefactor who endowed the almshouses, John Sleddall, was a descendant of Kendal's first alderman in 1636. There is a tradition that John Sleddall originally intended to build the almshouses in the village of New Hutton, but having been kept waiting in a draughty passage by the vicar to discuss the matter he took umbrage and moved the project to Kendal. A good view of the Victorian Gothic chapel is to be seen looking west from the towpath.

The former chapel of the Sleddall Almshouses seen from the towpath

PARKSIDE ROAD CEMETARY

Where the towpath meets Parkside Road there is an entrance to the town's principal cemetery, laid out in 1854 by George Webster, with a pair of Gothic chapels and ornate crocketed iron gates and railings. An elaborate set of walks catered for the Victorian taste for promenades amongst the tombstones and the many trees planted beside them have now grown into a mature and varied arboretum. The cemetery is divided by Parkside Road into two areas, one to the north for members of the Established Church and Catholics, and one to the south for Dissenters. Later commentators have speculated as to whether they are separated widely enough to avoid spiritual contamination!

WATERCROOK ROMAN FORT

In a loop of the River Kent, in a field below the point where the towpath crosses from the east to the west side of the Natland Road, lies the Roman Fort of Watercrook. It forms a low platform of about one and a half hectares with part of a rampart and some ditches still discernible. Former excavations revealed a gatehouse and guardrooms and pottery finds dated the site to mainly second century occupation. It is privately owned.

SEDGWICK AQUEDUCT

The skew or angled aqueduct on which the canal crosses the main road through Sedgwick village is believed to have been designed by the great John Rennie (1761-1821), a civil engineer who trained under James Watt. This considerable architectural and engineering design achievement was the first of its type to be built in the country and possibly the only one to be constructed in the canal era. It enjoys the status of a Scheduled Ancient Monument. Access from the aqueduct to street level is down a flight of steps.

On the offside of the canal channel are four wheelwright's hooping stones. Cart wheels were placed on the stones, the heated iron rims were then fitted onto them and doused with water to contract them to a tight fit on the wheels.

The Sedgwick Aqueduct   *British Waterways*

Sedgwick House   *Stephen Appleby*

SEDGWICK HOUSE

The Victorian mansion seen from the towpath on Sedgwick Hill was the
home of the Wakefield family, locally well known in connection with
the Mary Wakefield Music Festival. The house, built in the Victorian
Perpendicular manner in 1868-1869 was designed by Paley and Austin.

SEDGWICK GUNPOWDER WORKS

The former widespread woodlands on the thinner soils of the South
Lake District supported numerous small woodland crafts and industries,
the main products being oak bark for tanning and charcoal. Charcoal
was the main ingredient for gunpowder manufacture and a small
diversion from the towpath on Sedgwick Hill leading to the wooded
gorge below takes the visitor to a former gunpowder-manufacturing site.
Crossing the road bridge and following first the road and then the
footpath on the west side of the River Kent upstream leads to the ruins
of the New Sedgwick Gunpowder Works. The location will be
recognised by a group of large rocky outcrops in the river.

Charcoal was made mainly from oak and birch stems cut down as coppice wood at fourteen-year intervals. Sedgwick was also able to obtain 'savins' or juniper wood from which the finest gunpowder was made. The Sedgwick site had the benefit of the nearby port of Milnthorpe through which saltpetre could be imported from India and sulphur from Italy. It also had the water power of the River Kent available for the crushing and grinding mills and had a supporting industry of barrel-making at Milnthorpe.

The Kendal entrepreneur and Quaker, John Wakefield, built his first gunpowder mill here in 1764 and in the local trade directory of 1829 was said to be producing about eighty barrels of powder a week. Nothing of this mill, which was on the east bank of the River Kent, survives today but in 1799 Wakefield bought another gunpowder works at Low Wood on the west side of the River Kent and by 1849 had increased production to about two hundred and fifty barrels of gunpowder a week. This was mainly blasting powder used in mining and quarrying but gunpowder was also one of the commodities exchanged in the slave trade. As some of the Sedgwick gunpowder was sold for military use, John Wakefield was excluded from the Society of Friends.

Ruins of Larkrigg Gunpowder Works   *Leslie Leak*

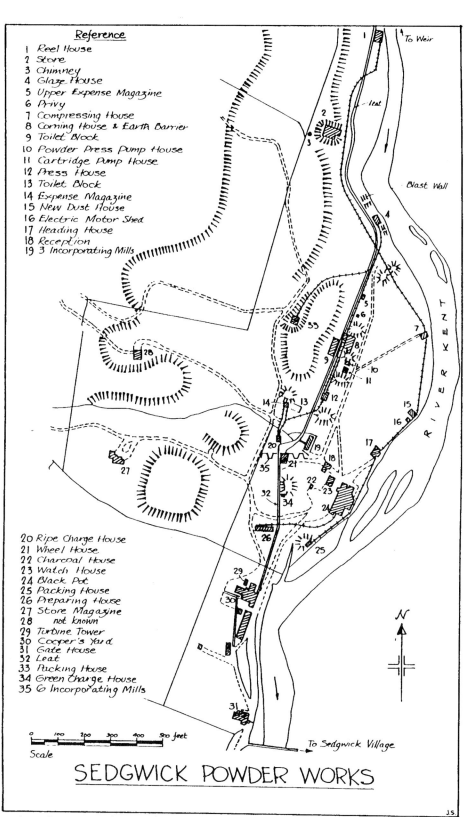

Reference
1 Reel House
2 Store
3 Chimney
4 Glaze House
5 Upper Expense Magazine
6 Privy
7 Compressing House
8 Corning House & Earth Barrier
9 Toilet Block
10 Powder Press Pump House
11 Cartridge Pump House
12 Press House
13 Toilet Block
14 Expense Magazine
15 New Dust House
16 Electric Motor Shed
17 Heading House
18 Reception
19 3 Incorporating Mills

20 Ripe Charge House
21 Wheel House
22 Charcoal House
23 Watch House
24 Black Pot
25 Packing House
26 Preparing House
27 Store Magazine
28   not known
29 Turbine Tower
30 Cooper's Yard
31 Gate House
32 Leat
33 Packing House
34 Green Charge House
35 6 Incorporating Mills

Scale

SEDGWICK POWDER WORKS

Sedgwick Gunpowder Works.   *Courtesy of E M Patterson and J Simmons*

In 1850 John Wakefield moved the Sedgwick works to Gatebeck and remains of the tramway from Gatebeck, which crossed the canal at Crooklands are still to be seen. The gunpowder was hauled along the tramway by horses shod with brass shoes to avoid striking sparks.

In 1857 a new proprietor opened a new gunpowder works at Sedgwick on the west bank of the river, Wakefield retiring the following year. The site is now owned by the National Trust and is occupied in the summer months by a Caravan Club and is accessible to the public only by prior arrangement. Amongst the features still visible are the mill race, the saltpetre house, the refining sheds, offices and the ruins of other buildings illustrated on the previous page, all dispersed through the two thousand feet length of the site (For details see 'Blackpowder Manufacture in Cumbria' by E M Patterson (38)). The site was again used for storing ammunition in World War II.

The Westmorland trade directory for 1849, commenting on the Sedgwick gunpowder mill, observed, '*An explosion occasionally takes place, which may be heard at a considerable distance, but without occasioning any loss of life.*' Although perhaps true at the time, employees were not so fortunate at later dates. A report prepared for the Home Secretary on an explosion at the press house at Gatebeck in 1881, describes the incident, '*Scarcely one stone was left standing on another,*' part of the roof was thrown to a distance of fifty-seven yards and part of the heavy pressing equipment to fifty yards. Many of the surrounding trees, which were forty to fifty feet high, were shorn off, blown out of the ground or stripped of their limbs. Of the two workmen in the building one was blown to pieces and the body of the other was hurled a distance of twenty-two yards. No conclusion was reached on the cause of the explosion.

Traditionally, miners and quarrymen prepared their blasting charges at home after the day's work simply by putting a measure of loose blasting powder into a paper bag, inserting a fuse and pasting down the bag. It was not unusual for this to be done by the family sitting around a table, by candlelight and often by an open fire. The resulting frequent accidents led to the Explosions Act of 1875, which required charges to be prepared at designated factory premises where the cartridges were pressed under a hydraulic ram. Notwithstanding the Explosives Act, explosions still occurred, one at the Sedgwick works in 1883 killing three men. One wall of the building was blown out, the roof was blown off to a height of at least fifty feet and bits of cartridge boxes, moulds, and powder barrels were reduced to debris and scattered in all directions to a distance of sixty-five yards.

In 1906 a pressing house at Sedgwick was ignited when a nearby tree was struck by lightning. Not only was it entirely destroyed but a piece of burning wood was blown onto another mill some seventy yards away causing that too to explode. In the same years the glazing house and corning (granulating) mill exploded with the loss of three lives, the reports on these incidents disclosing that no less than thirty-eight mills had exploded at Sedgwick since 1877. The works closed in 1935.

HINCASTER TUNNEL

This spectacular specimen of canal architectural engineering, 378 yards long, is a compromise structure allowing barges to be hand hauled along chains set in the tunnel wall while the horses were led around the gentle inclines of a sunken path curving around the foot of a hill. A report to a meeting early in 1815 describes the early stages of the work:

Hincaster Tunnel   *British Waterways*

'The deep cutting at both ends of Hincaster Tunnel is proceeding and the Excavation of the Tunnel is let. Much difficulty has arisen in endeavouring to procure stone for the Arching of this Tunnel, Limestone being the only stone within many miles of the work, and the quarries not yielding material of necessary dimensions without very great expense, your Committee have some thoughts of arching the Tunnel with brick.'

After citing some precedents for brickwork tunnels the report continues:

'Within a short distance of the Tunnel (below Moss Side Farm near Heversham in fact), clay may be got... ...and the bricks which have been made from it have met with the approbation of the engineers...'

A year later 350,000 bricks had been made and the following year the tunnel was constructed with the first ten yards at either end built in stone and the remainder in brick. The tunnel is three hundred and seventy-eight yards long and used over two million bricks. Ten thousand bricks left over from the tunnel, were put up for sale in 1818 by Thomas Fletcher, the canal engineer.

TEWITFILD LOCKS

The Northern Reaches end at Tewitfield in a flight of eight locks, built to lift the canal some 76 feet over three quarters of a mile and completed in 1818. These are wide locks constructed by Thomas Fletcher, the canal engineer, to accommodate small sea going vessels which came in from the Irish Sea via Glasson Dock. Much research into the feasibility of restoring the Northern Reaches has been carried out in the last thirty years, one of the major obstacles being the M6 Motorway which blocks off the canal a short distance above the upper lock. The solution proposed is to take the canal under the motorway at the level of the lock below this and construct a new lock on the upper side of the motorway. With the help of Lottery funding work is expected to begin around 2005.

WOODS AND HEDGES

Beyond the southern limits of Kendal the canal embankment supports a variety of small woodlands and hedgerows, some of them planted when the canal was constructed and some naturally regenerated. For the

Tewitfield Locks. *British Waterways*

Larkrigg Wood. View from the towpath

towpath walker particularly, they contribute a major element of the canal side experience variously defining the limits of the canal banks and opening up to allow views of the wider landscape.

Wherever it has not been actively or intensively managed, self sown and self regenerating native woodland has colonised the canal banks, ash and sycamore being the most aggressive invaders. Where the topography provides for a 'flushed' drainage with soil nutrients washing in from

Horse Park Bridge with relics of a former hawthorn hedge

higher ground the woodland has often an under-storey of hazel, a ground flora with Dog's Mercury locally dominant and wild cherry amongst the larger trees. On slopes where the soil nutrients tend to be leached the species composition is often poorer with Dog's Mercury sparse or absent. Many of the ancient hedges have merged with the bank-side woodland to give a high proportion of hawthorn. Although no longer an effective hedgerow, ancient individual trees produce nesting sites and, in season, abundant food for a variety of insects, birds and small mammals.

A particular type of nutrient-rich native woodland is encountered at Larkrigg Wood, north of Sedgwick, where the canal bed passes through an ancient coppice wood, coppiced or felled for charcoal production on a fourteen-year rotation by the woodland tenant. In the Manor of Levens the mature standards remained unfelled and were left to grow as timber at the discretion of the Lord of the Manor. The shallow soil over the local limestone yields a rich and varied ground flora with luxuriant Dog's Mercury and old mossy walls, home to a great variety of native molluscs. The tree canopy arches over the towpath to create a special enclosed woodland experience.

A quite different kind of canal-side woodland is the amenity planting of larch trees, the plantations if not the individual trees contemporary with the period of canal construction. Most of the old stone bridges have a few larches beside them creating the 'picturesque' effect so

Sedgwick Hill Bridge with amenity planting of larch and beech

Natland Park. Stumps from a former larch plantation.

popular in the early 19th century. These small groups are generally on rising ground above canal level and though generally of larch, described by Wordsworth as a tree of 'singular beauty', in some locations included beeches as at the crest of Sedgwick Hill.

The plantings are generally too small to have any value as timber although some may have been used for temporary repairs to the canal banks. There are some long narrow strips of ancient larch wood besides the towpath at Crooklands, which are certainly of 'singular beauty' where they overhang the canal.

Canal bank amenity planting. Larch trees beside Barkers' Lane Bridge, Farleton.

Chapter Thirteen

THE FUTURE

Following years of decay and neglect the canal's future took a more hopeful turn in 1992 when Scott Wilson Kirkpatrick published an engineering study commissioned by the Inland Waterways Association. It showed that despite the obstacles of the M6 and A6070 road crossing and the infilling of two miles of the canal at the Kendal end, it was technically feasible to bring the Northern Reaches back into water. The many aspects considered by the study included the quantity and quality of the water, which could be supplied to the canal by its streams; the restoration and remedial works needed along the entire length of the earthworks; the condition of the 52 Westmorland limestone arch bridges, aqueducts, locks, tunnels and other structures; and the obstructions created by road crossings, service mains and sewers. The estimated cost of the project was thirty million pounds.

In 1998 the Government published another report entitled 'Waterways Restoration Priorities' which set out a ranking priority list for waterway restoration schemes. It described the Lancaster Canal scheme as 'An important heritage canal restoration which, coupled with the provision of the Ribble Link, will re-extend the northern limit of the national connected system, foreshortened at Tewitfield by the building of the M6 Motorway, and so enhance the recreational and economic state of the rural corridor northwards to Kendal and into the Lake District.' Against this background British Waterways identified the Lancaster Canal as 'one of five medium term priority schemes of regional significance' and in March 2000 published its prospectus for restoring the Northern Reaches (39). It perceives the scheme as bringing benefits not only to the Northern Reaches themselves but as a potent instrument of regeneration of the urban centres traversed further south.

Recognising the massive funding required, the prospectus defines the benefits of the scheme as 'Providing a new focus and catalyst for regeneration of formerly derelict areas of our towns and cities; opening up the tourism and leisure potential of the network of canal corridors for both formal and informal recreation; and introducing enhanced scope for water based alternative and innovative approaches to sustainable transportation strategies.' The prospectus proceeds to define these transcendental aspirations in terms of job creation; reduction of traffic congestion on the roads; opportunities for constructing hotels, offices and houses on canal-side locations; leisure attractions including new marinas; conservation of the ecology of the canal and restoration of its structures. The potential for debating the figures estimated is considerable.

The prospectus lays out a timetable for the project with preparation of a conservation plan, design work, land assembly and fund-raising in the first four years and construction beginning in the fifth. Preliminary work on the conservation plan has already begun. Meanwhile the Lancaster Canal Trust, a voluntary body which has been lobbying for the preservation of the canal since the 1960s continues to champion the restoration of what is undoubtedly the most attractive canal route in the country.

Artist's impression of the proposed Kendal Canal Head basin
Courtesy British Waterways

REFERENCES

1) Marshall, J D & M Davies-Shiel, 1977. The Historical Archeology of the Lake Counties. Michael Moon. 2nd edn.

2) Curwen, J F 1917. The Lancaster Canal. Trans. C & W Ant. & Arch. Soc. XVII, 26-47.

3) Bingham, R 1995. Kendal – A Social History. Cicerone Press.

4) Wilson, P N 1968. Canal Head, Kendal. Trans. C & W Ant & Arch. Soc. LXIII, 132-150.

5) Wilson P N 1975 Gilkes' 1853 to 1975. 122 years of Water Turbine and Pump Manufacture. Trans. Newcomen Soc. 47, 73-84.

6) Porter, R 1982. English Society in the Eighteenth Century. Penguin Books.

7) Hardcastle, P 1998. Canals roots and routes, www.canalroutes.

8) Cameron, A 1996. Slate from Coniston. A history of the Coniston Slate Industry. Cumbria Amenity Trust Mining History Soc. 151pp.

9) Parson, W & W White, 1829. History, Directory and Gazetteer of the Counties of Cumberland and Westmorland. Baines, Leeds.

10) Mannex, P J 1849. History, Topography and Directory of Westmorland.

11) Bulmer, T F 1885. History, Topography and Directory of Westmorland.

12) Curwen, J F 1900. Kirkbie Kendall. Titus Wilson, Kendal.

13) Philpotts, R 1983. Building the Lancaster Canal. Blackwater Books, London.

14) Nicholson, C 1832. The Annals of Kendal. 1st edn.

15) Bottomley, M Pers. Comm. From notes of a conversation with Maurice Day 1978.

16) Peter Crewdson, Pers. Comm.

17) Links, W L 1968. Notes on the Origins of the Tobacco and Snuff Industry in Kendal. Typescript. CRO/WDB 14.

18) Boumphrey, R S *et al.* 1975. An Armorial for Westmorland and Lonsdale CWAAS.

19) Bouch, C M L & G P Jones. 1961. A Short Economic and Social History of the Lake Counties 1500-1830. Manchester University Press.

20) Wilson, P N 1968. Westmorland Gazette 13th Sept.

21) Anon. 1855. Westmorland Gazette & Kendal Advertiser 4th Aug.

22) Wilson, Joanna. 1989. Report prepared for Goodacre Carpets.

23) Philip Edwards. Pers. Comm.

24) Smith, A H 1967. The Place Names of Westmorland.

25) Cumbria Record Office/WDB/35/107

26) Blake Tyson. Pers. Comm.

27) Cumbria Record Office/WDX 708/T46

28) The Year Book of Facts in Science and Art 1839. Simpkin Marshall, London.

29) Cumbria Record Office/WDG 14/278 87.

30) The Websters of Kendal, Exhib Catalogue 1973. Cumbria Record Office.

31) Peter Crewdson. Pers. Comm.

32) David, R G 1981. The Icehouses of Cumbria. Trans C & W Ant. & Arch. Soc. LXXXI, p137.

33) Somervell, J 1930. Water-Power mills of South Westmorland. Titus Wilson, Kendal.

34) Marshall, J D. 1975. Kendal 1661-1801. The Growth of the Modern Town. C & W Ant. & Arch. Soc. and The Curwen Trust.

35) Satchell, J E & O Wilson, 1988. Christopher Wilson of Kendal. Kendal Civic Society & Frank Peters Publishing.

36) Cumbria Record Office, Kendal Papers.

37) Cumbria Record Office, Westmorland Notebook.

38) Patterson, E M & Jack Simmons, 1995. Blackpowder Manufacture in Cumbria. Faversham Society. Faversham Papers No 43 pp 32-37.

39) Lancaster Canal. Gateway to the Lake District. A Prospectus. BritishWaterways. March 2000.

40) Keates, Tony 1999. Lime burning on Kendal Fell. The Cumbria Industrialist. Vol. 2, pp 32-49.

41) Taylor, Angus. The Websters of Kendal. In preparation.